MW00584076

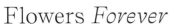

Flowers *Forever*

Flowers
Forever

Celebrate the Beauty of Dried
Flowers with Stunning Floral Art

Bex Partridge

Hardie Grant

BOOKS

Photography by Laura Edwards

Contents

Introduction

My Journey   6
The Beauty Is in the Decay   10

How Does Your Garden Grow?   17

How to Grow a Garden Full of Dried Flowers   18
The Best of Both Worlds: Annuals & Perennials   20
The Wonder of Wildflowers   24
Year-Round Harvesting   25
Reimagining the Lawn   26
My Greenhouse   29
Collecting Seeds: Going Full Circle   30
A Conscious Garden   33

From Fresh to Dried   39

What, When & How to Dry   40
    True Everlastings   45
    For Interest   53
    For Height   58
    To Fill   65
    From the Wild   71
    Berries, Grasses & Seedheads   79
    Shrubs & Foliage   91
    Tricky Folk   100

Creating With Dried Flowers   **109**

On Colour   110
On Fragrance   114
On Flow   117
Sourcing Your Blooms   118
Leave No Trace   123
The Need for Natural Materials   127

Dried Flower Designs   **133**

Seeking Out Inspiration   134
Spring Branches   138
Flowers on Fabric   144
Verdant Wreath   151
A Summer Meadow   157
Colour Play   164
A Table Full of Everlasting Love   171
Creating Drama & Scale   177
Autumn Harvest   185
Three Ways with Vessels   191
The Cloud   201
Winter Solstice   209

About the Author & Acknowledgements   218
Resources   220
Index   221

My Journey

One of the unexpected outcomes of the COVID-19 pandemic for so many of us was that it afforded us a deeper appreciation of the natural world, whether as a result of spending more time outside or the slower pace of life. This temporary pause allowed us to stop and take notice of each and every bud of hope that appeared during the bright, nurturing spring of the UK's first lockdown. My garden – and my approach to gardening – has always been led by and in harmony with nature, but that spring shifted something in me and made me realise the importance of the way we choose to live our lives. With endless weeks at home, I discovered the joy of drying tulips, peonies and ranunculus. As my flowers and garden became my safe place, as well as giving me the gift of escapism from the increasing stresses of everyday life, I experimented and created more than I ever have before and began to break down the walls I had built around the idea of drying flowers.

This is when *Flowers Forever* was fully conceptualised – from a meeting in London with my Publisher in the weeks before we were locked down, to writing and growing during the darkest depths of the restrictions in preparation for the final book. It has been brought to life at a time in our lives when nothing is as it was before, and at a time when my family and I went through one of the biggest changes we have ever made.

Spurred on by the temporary change in our pace of life and with more time to access nature, as life in our busy town came to a halt we made the decision as a family to move to a more rural location offering space and tranquillity. Leaving behind our home town dwelling and settling in the depths of the lush green hills of East Devon, in the south of the UK, has been the best decision we ever made. This move has allowed me to go from growing my flowers in a small, yet incredibly productive town garden and allotment, to growing in a wild half-acre of fertile soil. The space has really elevated my growing capacity and capabilities and also further increased my knowledge of working with dried materials.

It has inspired my work immensely and with a studio in the garden, nestled under a gathering of mature trees, I spend hours and hours out there each day focused on my work.

Flowers Forever was my creative constant throughout the turbulent year of 2020, a beautiful project to focus on and to challenge me and my imagination. Many of the designs in these pages were imagined in the days spent out in my cabin studio watching the seasons change around me, and with nowhere to go and no one to see, I was able to focus all my efforts on creating this book.

With *Flowers Forever* I want to share the complete process involved in my work, from the sowing of seeds and the nurturing of the soil, through to the growing and harvesting, and finally putting together my designs. My aim is to leave as little impact as possible on this precious world and, where I can, use my practices to give back in exchange for that which I take. I am strict with my values and I will always stay true to them in the way that I garden, source materials and create my designs. With *Flowers Forever* I want to showcase these values and how they come together to form a constant thread throughout my projects. I am so grateful that I get to call this work, that my hands and mind are busy every day with the fruits of the natural world and that, on any given day, I can be growing or drying or creating something from the land on which we live. I know how very lucky I am.

In this book I will share the breadth and depth of my knowledge – as it stands – of flowers and foliage to dry, including my approach to growing. I aim to inspire you and show you how to work with materials throughout the seasons to lift your home environment or special occasion by creating sustainable, long-lasting installations. By working with the seasons and reflecting the outside world with everything I create, I hope to show you how to bring the outside in and how to sit a little closer to the natural world.

The Beauty Is in the Decay

I love nothing more than to change a person's opinion about dried flowers. For many there is still a huge amount of negativity around them, and I do understand why – after all, there is a fine line between a modern, visually captivating creation and a staid, dull and dusty display best suited to a dark corner of the house or perhaps even the compost heap. For this reason I'm conscious when working with dried flowers that I continue to push my designs to ensure they stay fresh and enticing, and challenge people's expectations and beliefs.

Dried flowers can be dramatic and awe-inspiring, particularly for those who haven't experienced them before. I continue to be amazed by how fascinated people can be by flowers in this form. The beauty is in their decay, in their translucent petals that catch the light and their soft kaleidoscope of colours and textures. Nature belies belief, especially when preserved in this way.

There have been studies showing that stopping and noticing small (and enjoyable) aspects of the natural world activates the para-sympathetic element of our autonomic nervous system. This is the opposite of the sympathetic responses which include our flight-and-fight response and, for many, is the default state. It seems flowers and nature in any form can help us to pause and calm ourselves just by the simple act of observing them. I see this reaction when visitors come to my studio. I watch them visibly relax when they step through the door, pausing by each and every flower head to take a closer look and marvel at all the beauty and wonder. Of course, this response is not unique to dried flowers, although perhaps it's magnified by the fact that these flowers are preserved to be enjoyed forever more.

Opposite

VARIETY: Iceland poppy *(Papaver nudicaule)* in a state of decay

I think it is safe to say that dried flowers are no longer a 'trend'. They are, in fact, forming an important part of the slow flowers movement. It's been incredibly encouraging to watch people's acceptance and understanding of dried flowers grow over the past few years, to see them evolve from something relatively niche (or 'on trend', depending upon how you view things!) to something that is now widely accepted and sought after. With the world in such a state of flux from an environmental, political and societal perspective, and the fact that we are still feeling the impact of the pandemic as I write, more and more of us have a heightened awareness of the origins of the things we buy and bring into our homes. After food, flowers in all their forms are the next in line to be scrutinised by huge swathes of people who are awakening to the realisation that the way we have been consuming in recent years is simply unsustainable. We know that fresh flowers are scarce in the depths of winter, but that doesn't mean we can't enjoy flowers throughout this season.

Dried flowers for many are not being sought out as a replacement for fresh flowers. I adore a bunch of fresh flowers as much as anyone else (although I admit to mostly going on to dry them). Dried flowers are an interior design choice for the savvy and nature-inspired collective, a way to add texture and tones to a living space, and can be considered as a purchase in much the same way as a piece of art or an artisan cushion would be.

When featured at events or used to soften and enhance retail and restaurant spaces, dried flowers are chosen by businesses who can see the value they bring from both an aesthetic as well as a longevity perspective. It's about offering the fullest sensory experience possible.

Opposite

VARIETY: Garden dahlia drying in the warm sun

Overleaf (Left and right)

VARIETY: Ox-eye daisy *(Leucanthemum vulgare)* and winged everlasting *(Ammobium alatum)*

Sustainability and Longevity

Sustainability is a big word and one that is being used more and more by businesses and organisations who want to show they are doing the 'right thing'. It can be a bit of minefield to work out what is genuinely sustainable and where a business is 'greenwashing' (giving the impression that they are concerned about the environment, even if their actions actually harm the environment). Unfortunately, even in the world of flowers, both fresh and dried, there is a lack of transparency as well as understanding around the eco credentials of plant materials. Given that flowers are a natural product, it's perfectly understandable for us to assume they are inherently sustainable, but that isn't always the case. In much the same way as with our food, we need to consider how they're grown, flown, packaged and then sometimes tampered with (see *The Need for Natural Materials*, pages 127–130).

However, if grown, dried and sourced in a responsible, considered way, dried flowers can be one of the most sustainable flower products on the market. They offer a long-lasting, natural means of decorating our homes, events and shared spaces.

How Does Your Garden Grow?

How to Grow a Garden Full of Dried Flowers

I've been gardening for as long as I can remember and growing flowers to dry for a good many years. With every season I experience, my learning continues. My knowledge of what and how to grow, which materials dry well, the best times for picking to dry, and the most effective combinations of flowers for the garden and for displays increases, year on year. This is the life of anyone who chooses to garden – a cyclical learning journey, one where nature will continue to surprise, delight and at times frustrate us with her unpredictable ways. It provides much excitement and encourages adaptability and creativity to overcome unknowns and unexpected challenges. Gardening is also an act of mindfulness. The days I start and end in my garden knee-deep in soil are the best. I couldn't be without it.

Growing my own plant materials to work with helps to keep me and my designs rooted in the natural world. It gifts me a deeper appreciation for the plants I grow and guides me on how to weave together flower and foliage combinations that are reminiscent of scenes from the great outdoors. I grow exactly what I want, whether that be a spindly stem of a *Sanguisorba* or the rich tones of *Amaranthus cordatus* 'Hot Biscuits', and the joy that comes when my endeavours are successful is immense. Even when the world appears to be falling apart around us, the garden keeps on growing and keeps on giving. A constant in an ever-changing world.

I've been so inspired by the unspoilt scenery that surrounds us here in Devon that I have embraced a much wilder and more natural style of gardening. While I have turned a small area over to growing annuals and vegetables, the rest I have left as natural as possible for aesthetic reasons and to increase the biodiversity, foregoing mowing for tapestry lawns and allowing our garden's boundaries to grow upwards and develop into a natural hedgerow. All of this with the aim of maintaining our precious eco-systems and welcoming more wildlife in.

VARIETY: *Centaurea cyanus* 'Classic Magic' and white and yellow forms of strawflower *(Helichrysum bracteatum)*

The Best of Both Worlds: Annuals & Perennials

When I first began growing flowers to dry, I focused on annuals and the stalwart varieties of everlastings. I grew armfuls of strawflowers and statice alongside *Nigella* and cornflowers. I cultivated plants that grew in volume and would give me plentiful harvests within the year. Now, I'm also focusing on growing more unusual flowers, including perennials and more tricky annuals. I've learned that while traditional everlastings are an absolute must-have, they are happier when mixed with a wilder, softer bunch of companions, just as they would in the garden.

Perennials also offer security throughout the growing year – with weather patterns becoming more extreme due to climate change, perennials can withstand such fluctuations in a way that annuals can't.

This desire for a wider variety of dried flowers to work with has very much informed my planting design. That, coupled with the desire for a garden that holds year-round interest and useful plant material, has resulted in a diverse growing space that draws upon the best of both annuals and perennials.

Annuals: It's All About the Show

Annuals are plants that germinate, flower and set seed all within one year, with growth coming the next year from the previous year's seed. They are labour-intensive throughout the majority of their life and require dedication and lots of energy. So in any one year of growing, I have to get from seed to harvest in a matter of months. This involves sowing the seed, pricking out, hardening off and, finally, planting out. After which, regular watering and deadheading ensues, as annuals can rarely be left unattended and, to flourish, require the right amount of water, heat and light. Yet after all that hard work done, I'm rewarded with armfuls of flowers throughout the summer and my cabin rapidly fills up with drying blooms from then onwards. All the hard work of the earlier months of the year are forgotten and a sense of pride washes over me, knowing that I grew each and every one of these blooms myself.

When growing annuals, it is worth considering where they will be situated within the garden. I used to grow annuals on my allotment and my garden was reserved for perennials. Here, in Devon, I have positioned my annual beds at the far end of the garden. There, in the summer, I can see the billowing clouds of flowers, and in the winter the area is tucked away out of sight. The reason for this is that for a large portion of the year the beds will be bare soil once the annuals have been pulled out for harvesting. This space gets full sun during the main growing months and in the depths of winter, when light does not matter, sits in dappled shade.

ANNUALS FOR BEGINNERS:

Love in the mist *Nigella* – for the flowers and seedheads
Annual everlasting (*Xeranthemum annuum*)
Poppy (*Papaver*) – for the seedheads
Strawflower (*Helichrysum bracteatum*)
Statice (*Limonium sinuatum*)

The Power of Perennials

I discovered and truly appreciated the immense beauty of perennials a few years ago after a trip to a garden in Norfolk, on the east coast of the UK, which was created by the Dutch garden designer Piet Oudf. I was blown away by the textures and tones all swaying softly as one in the light breeze, lit up by the low September sun. Here was a garden in early autumn that looked better now than in the summer. That garden sparked an interest in me and opened my eyes to the vast array of possibilities for planting and drying plant materials.

Much of what I saw in the beds had already begun to dry itself in the early autumn sun after months of growth and effort. The grasses were a jumbled mix and statuesque seedheads shot up past them as they reached for the sky. Inspired by the garden, I had visions of a planting space that allowed me to pick directly from the plant when needed and create designs from it throughout the year. Until we moved to our rural home, replicating this style of perennial planting was a challenge as it's better suited to larger areas, and my bijoux town garden just did not provide enough space. So, when we acquired a bigger garden, one of the first areas I planted up was my perennial flower bed, bringing carloads of plants with me from my previous garden and allotment. This growing space sits right up close to the house, splitting our garden in two to allow for intrigue, and has been designed to hold interest all year round. I've selected plants and grasses that work well for drying and will provide months of soft-hued vistas from our back windows. I have avoided, for the most part, traditional cottage garden plants (besides the ones that were already in situ) and opted instead for those whose foliage and seedheads remain intact through the year.

While I try to grow most of my perennials from seed, it can be a slow process so I occasionally buy established plants from local growers. However, there are other low-cost ways to source perennials. I have acquired many beautiful specimens from neighbours and friends over the years, as many perennials can be divided and replanted in other locations in spring and autumn, before the hard growth kicks in.

MY FAVOURITE PERENNIALS:

Bergamot (*Monarda*)

Catmint (*Nepeta*)

Globe thistle (*Echinops*)

Feverfew (*Tanacetum parthenium*)

Goldenrod (*Solidago*)

Purple top (*Verbena bonariensis*)

Sea holly (*Eryngium*)

Yarrow (*Achillea*)

The Wonder of Wildflowers

While many wonderful wildflowers can be dried, I try as much as possible to limit those that I take from wild spaces. Wildflowers are much better left where they are growing naturally, to increase biodiversity and play their part in our all-important ecosystem. There are also many guidelines stating what can and can't be taken from the wild (see page 71), so please do be responsible and research what is and is not permitted in your local area before picking any wildflowers or foraging for plant material.

In an attempt to become more self sufficient, I am slowly adding more wildflowers to my garden, always native and ones that I know work well for drying as well as being beneficial for wildlife. I've got to know what grows well here by studying the hedgerows that line our road and have then added those flowers to the already exciting mix of wildflowers growing freely in our soil. I have an exuberant periwinkle that is clambering over everything, weaving its web of tough roots wherever it spreads. So each year I'm stripping back a section that resides along the banked edges of the garden to free up the soil and am embarking upon planting wildflowers there. When wildflowers find their happy place they will freely self-seed year after year, although as with many native wildflowers, they tend to flower in the second year of sowing, so patience is required.

WILDFLOWERS I'M GROWING IN MY GARDEN:

Evening primrose (*Oenothera biennis*)
Goldenrod (*Solidago*)
Teasel (*Dipsacus*)

Year-Round Harvesting

Moving to a rural location with fields, woodlands and road verges surrounding me, much of which is left untouched by the council and local farmers, has given me a real insight into what types of plant materials overwinter well and can be picked during those dark months of autumn and winter. Although I have lived most of my life in busy town centres where everything, including road verges, gardens and parks are maintained to the nth degree, I feel much more at home in this unkempt wilderness – it suits me and inspires my work. On a dark day, when life feels heavy, taking a walk around the garden to see what I can find to work with helps me to feel grounded and reminds me how giving the natural world is.

Taking inspiration from the wild, I avoid the big cutbacks that we are advised to do in the garden at certain points in the year and instead leave most seedheads and leaves to die back on the plant. This simple act has allowed me to discover many different plant materials that overwinter well and are suitable for drying. Many of the perennials I've planted are happy to have their seedheads and stalks left in place, benefiting not only my work but also the wildlife in our garden.

Allowing foliage to die and draw back into the soil and leaving seedheads in situ where insects can take shelter during the colder months is vitally important. Once the warmer weather returns in spring, I wait until the outside temperatures are a solid and consistent 10°C (50°F) before cutting back, to allow those insects overwintering in the diapause stage of their lives to wake up from their slumber. If there are areas that I must clear before the temperature rises, then I will wrap any long-spent stems in bundles and leave them on the side until the days are warmer to give any insects a chance to wake up and start their new life.

Reimagining the Lawn

The bright green, monotone lawns that are synonymous with British gardens are a relatively recent trend and one that I have in the past fully embraced. Mowing the lawn used to be a much-loved ritual of mine and would often be the first thing I did when we returned home from a holiday. Recently, I've started to explore the idea of the lawn having a different purpose, partly out of necessity, as I simply don't have the time to mow the expanse of lawn, and partly out of a desire to provide a richer habitat for insects and birds. I am slowly turning our lawn into a mosaic of herbs, wildflowers, bulbs and a mix of native grasses of differing swards. The chickens help to keep the length of the grass down as they graze their way across the land, which in turn allows the wildflowers and various grasses to flourish. I grow other native plants from seed to intersperse with what is already there and in the autumn plant naturalising spring bulbs to burst forth and slowly fill the space. Much of what I plant will go on to be picked for drying and to be used in my smaller work.

These types of mixed-up lawns can also withstand weather extremes, reducing the need to turn the sprinkler on during the summer months, and the herbs and grasses dotted around provide colour and interest throughout the year as well as potential for food sources. A key plant to include in any wildflower lawn is yellow rattle, which outcompetes grasses and allows flowers to flourish.

PLANTS I'M FILLING MY LAWN WITH:

Oregano (*Origanum vulgare*)
Snake's head fritillary (*Fritillaria meleagris*)
Thyme (*Thymus vulgaris*)
Wild tulip (*Tulipa sylvestris*)

VARIETY: Bird's foot trefoil *(Lotus corniculatus)*, yarrow *(Achillea millefolium)* and tufted hair grass *(Deschampsia cespitosa)*

My Greenhouse

There really is something magical about greenhouses besides allowing your plants to get going earlier in the year. I have many a photo of me hunched over in my tiny greenhouse back home during the pandemic, sowing seeds of hope.

I love the unique earthy scent as I step into its calming space. A space where life springs forth after the long, dark winter days. Greenhouses are joyful and useful, and they are an important part in the journey of growing my plants from seed. My greenhouse allows me the opportunity to start my growing season earlier in the year and I am busy from mid-winter until late spring with sowings and pricking out. Many perennials will flower the year they're sown if the seeds enter the soil early enough, and starting annuals off in early autumn (for hardy varieties) and late winter for others (the varieties that can withstand it) allows successional sowing for increased harvests. Seeds really are magical – all they want to do is germinate and with a little bit of love and attention they will flourish.

The two main things that a greenhouse provides for seeds is light and warmth. My greenhouse has a lot of shelving, a big growing space, toughened glass, windows that open automatically when it gets too hot and an electric heater that runs using electricity from a renewable source, allowing me to sow earlier in the year. If you have limited space, then consider investing in a small portable greenhouse. But, if that's not possible, then a warm windowsill or conservatory will also work well.

This year, out of necessity, I have also used my greenhouse in the summer to quickly dry out plant material. Although plants can't stand too much time in a hot greenhouse, if monitored carefully, it can provide a great space for drying.

Collecting Seeds: Going Full Circle

Collecting seeds from the plants we grow makes sense. There is something deeply satisfying about growing next year's plants from this year's seeds. I am by no means an expert and tend to be haphazard in my seed-saving approach, but I have learned a few things:

Always collect on a dry day – this should ensure that the seeds are easily deposited from the seedhead when shaken.

If picking very ripe seedheads, use a big bowl to collect any seeds that fall from the main seedhead.

Collect seeds from the best of the best of your mother plants – this will hopefully ensure that they will be viable.

Label and date seed packets. Store your seeds in a cool, dry place until ready to sow and keep in mind that each year a seed's virility reduces.

PLANTS SUITED TO SAVING AND GROWING SEEDS:

Amaranth (*Amaranthus*)
Cornflower (*Centaurea cyanus*)
Flax (*Linum usitatissimum*)
Foxglove (*Digitalis*)
Honesty (*Lunaria annua*)
Love in the mist *Nigella*
Paper daisy (*Acrolinium*)
Strawflower (*Helichrysum bracteatum*)

I will often end up with a pile of swept-up seeds or bowls of mixed seeds from days when I've collected them in a rather disorganised fashion. I keep these and scatter them on a bare patch of soil once spring has arrived and the ground is warmer. I take a punt that something will come of it and rest easy knowing I haven't wasted a single precious seed.

VARIETY: Tulip seedheads

How Does Your Garden Grow?

A Conscious Garden

The COVID-19 pandemic and other large catastrophes have really brought home the importance of taking care of our world, and this has impacted how I grow and interact with my garden. I have learned a huge amount over the years and it is incredibly important that what and how I grow reflects my values. Many of the beliefs I held regarding how gardening should be done had to be untangled and learned again, to find a complementary approach that worked for both me and nature.

Some of the ways I do things and recommendations I share here may seem obvious, but I hope for the most part they will be inspiring. While I am by no means an expert on topics such as no-dig gardening and composting, it's well worth learning more about them and I have included resources on page 220 for you to do so.

No-Dig Gardening

I have been practising no-dig gardening for many years, inspired by a visit to the growing space of a friend of a flower farmer. There was not one single weed growing among her rows of abundant annuals.

The no-dig approach involves leaving the soil untouched every year. This allows the complex soil structure of microorganisms, mycelia, fungi and worms to remain intact. Nutrient-rich mulch is added to the top of existing beds each year to feed the soil in the same way fallen leaves and debris would nurture the soil in natural cycles. New beds can easily be created by laying cardboard (to smother grass and weeds) and topped with a thick layer of compost. These beds will be ready to plant in the same year they are created.

Besides limited soil disturbance, the other benefit of the no-dig method is the much-reduced prevalence of weeds. When soil is damaged by digging, seeds that have laid dormant burst forth into life to cover up the damaged soil. No-dig not only stops the weed seeds from being activated but the regular application of a layer of compost also smothers them, preventing them from growing – a vital time saver for any grower.

Compost

I always buy organic compost, ensuring it is peat-free. It is important to know that compost derived from peat (even if the supplier states that it has been sustainably managed) is damaging to our environment. Peaty fens are hugely important in capturing and storing carbon, with the ability to store five times more carbon than forested areas. That peat needs to stay in the ground, helping to sequester carbon.

There are some great non-peat alternatives on the market. I have used compost derived from the mushroom-growing industry and from seaweed, as well as from the council, who create compost from our garden waste. I recommend taking the time to seek out local alternatives to peat-based composts.

I am also learning to make my own compost. Everything from our food waste to old clothes, brown paper, cardboard and the chickens' waste goes onto our compost heaps. Adding any leftover materials from my work, also returns a lot of goodness to the soil and ensures plants that will grow into next year's dried flowers, so completing the cycle for me.

Chemical-Free Gardening

All my plants are grown using natural practices and without the use of chemicals. I do not use artificial fertilisers (I make my own seaweed fertilisers and have a wormery that produces plenty), aphid sprays or any other chemicals. These can upset the natural balance of the environment and in turn cause more problems than they seek to solve. Healthy ecosystems allow a garden to thrive which means that threats from disease and bugs can be tackled naturally.

We have a garden pond that is full to the brim with toads and newts

VARIETY: *Papaver rhoeas* 'Amazing Grey'

How Does Your Garden Grow?

which help to keep down the slug and snail population, and our chickens support in that way too. If I find a plant under attack from aphids, I will ask my boys to hunt out ladybirds and their larvae and pop them on the affected area. And where possible use companion planting to allow my plants to support each other's health.

Structures and Protection

I like my garden to look natural. To me, this means designing spaces that mould into their surroundings and minimising the use of plastics. It's also about finding alternatives to buying more 'things', both for budgetary reasons and also from a wider desire to consume less.

For example, when I need to create a fence, I'll utilise all the bits of wood I can find, hammering lengths of it directly into the ground and then fastening thinner sticks lengthways to allow me to fix chicken wire along the lower section. The chicken wire is always reused, whether in future design work or for fencing elsewhere.

To temporarily protect spaces where seeds have just been sown or plants freshly dug in, I make small, shallow barriers around the edge of the growing space using a tangle of intertwined twigs. Last winter we reduced our elderly hawthorn and then made protective structures with its thorny, lichen-covered branches.

To build a structure for climbing flowers and vegetables, I'll use hazel branches for the main structure with the smaller offshoots cut off, using these to form a natural matrix on which the vines can climb. If a bulb head is hanging or an annual drooping, I'll cut a small twig or stick from a plant that can take it and use that to offer support.

Harvesting Water

With weather patterns changing, harvesting and storing water for dry periods is becoming a necessity. Deep underneath our front garden is a subterranean water tank where we harvest and store rainwater. I also have water butts attached to my greenhouse, studio and garage.

From Fresh to Dried

What, When & How to Dry

One of the questions I get asked the most in relation to my work is 'What flowers are best for drying?' A few years ago, my answer would most likely have been the classics – strawflowers, statice and so on – but as my knowledge has grown, I find myself answering with: it really depends on your willingness to accept a flower as dried, not dead.

It comes down to aesthetics, predominantly. Let me explain what I mean by this. When we look at the more traditional varieties of dried flowers, such as strawflowers and their companions, their dried state doesn't differ hugely from that of their fresh. These are acceptable dried flowers to many as they look very similar to when they were fresh: bright in colour and structurally the same. When we look at flowers such as delphiniums, tulips or dahlias, however, there is a marked difference between their appearance when they are dried versus when they are fresh. In reality, there are very few flowers that won't dry but many whose appearance changes drastically when dried.

An important point to consider when drying a flower is whether it will be of much use at the end of the process. While it is true that nearly all flowers and foliage will dry in some form, it may be that they are not that useful when dried (for example, due to floppy stems).

While the likes of strawflowers and statice will retain their colour well when dried, I do find that they have a tendency to be brash, rigid and limiting when displayed on their own. This is why I combine them with the more unusual plants that I dry. What I grow is driven by what I want to use in my work and often out of necessity if I am unable to source what I need elsewhere. I get excited when the natural, softened petals and stems of more unusual perennials and shrubs I have grown elevate a dried flower display, giving it movement and a depth that the more traditional everlastings are unable to do on their own.

Over the following pages, you will find guides on how and when to dry individual plant materials, but it also comes down to learning to feel and assess the appearance of the flowers you want to dry. Much of this will come from experience and from your own trials, so I advise that when drying new materials you make a note of when they were picked and how they were dried (for how long, using which method, etc.,) so you can follow the same steps in the future or try another way if the results aren't as you had hoped.

When picking flowers for drying I consider the flowering time from bud to seedhead (for example, *Nigella* flowers quickly but rapidly loses its petals, requiring timely picking, whereas statice is much slower to flower and can be picked at varying stages of growth); their appearance; how they feel (for example, hydrangeas are ready to be picked when they begin to feel papery to the touch and have a lightness to them when held in your hand – they have a tendency to go floppy if picked too early and are tricky to revive); and if they continue to develop when drying (for example, strawflowers turn to seed if picked and hung too late in the process). For the most part it's a fine balance between picking too early and leaving it too late, so keep a keen eye on your plants and get to know each one's individual optimum picking time.

The condition of the stems you wish to dry is vitally important. In much the same was as you would condition a fresh flower before using it, flowers that are to be dried should be treated in the same way. While it is true that the best stems should be used, I would always suggest that you dry as many as possible. There is no point wasting a flower because of one slight imperfection.

Cut the stems with a clean pair of secateurs, strip any unwanted leaves from the stems and place the stems in a shallow bucket of water to stand overnight in a cool place. This will allow the plant material to have a good drink before it is hung out to dry. A beautiful plump stem that will hold its structure well as it goes through the drying process is better than one that has wilted before it has even gotten started.

Temperature

Keep flowers that are drying at a constant ambient room temperature. If the room is too cold, this may delay the drying process, which can affect their colour and appearance. And while some plants need a bit of extra warmth to dry well (such as dahlias), for the most part, long sustained periods of high temperatures will cause the flowers to become brittle and hard to work with.

Light

Light levels are important for colour retention. It is a good idea to dry your flowers in the dark. In saying that, I dry most of my flowers in my studio or garage as I like to watch them change from fresh to dry. So, while I don't stick to my own rule, I do ensure they are out of direct sunlight at the very least. When I want to achieve a natural bleached effect with *Ammi* and the like, I will often hang those stems in my greenhouse in the heat of summer to sear them dry.

Moisture

There are very few flowers and foliage that will dry successfully when exposed to high levels of moisture, so it's important that your drying space is as moisture-free as possible. I really can't stress enough how important a dry atmosphere is for your flowers. This is true for when they are on display too.

On the following pages, I share with you my favourite flowers to grow and dry. I have divided the blooms into groups that make sense to me and the way I use and work with them. There may, of course, be crossovers within the groupings and these are by no means hard-and-fast rules. I simply hope that they will help you to find alternative uses for your forever flowers.

Flowers Forever

True Everlastings

These are the flowers that come to mind for most people when they think of dried flowers. They are easy to grow, even easier to dry and retain their colour well. I am forever grateful for these varieties – they got me started on this journey of drying and I adore them both for the never-ending delight and colour they provide in the garden and their appeal in displays.

Most of the flowers in this section can be dried upside down in small bunches with their stems stripped bare. Many of them are annuals but if you live in a warmer climate with mild winters, it is possible to overwinter them with a little help from some horticultural fleece.

Strawflowers and other daisy-like everlastings are fantastic cut-and-come-again flowers and will keep producing blooms once picking commences. The same is true of statice and ammobium alatum, for example, although their stem length tends to reduce with each cutting.

VARIETY: (From left to right) *Nigella damascena* 'Albion Black Pod', curled dock *(Rumex crispus), Lonas inodora*, winged everlasting *(Ammobium alatum),* various *Helichrysum bracteatum* and mayweed *(Matricaria discoidea)*

Above

VARIETY: *Amaranthus cruentus* 'Hot Biscuits'

Opposite

VARIETY: Loves-lies-bleeding *(Amaranthus caudatus)*

Above

VARIETY: (Top) Annual everlasting *(Xeranthemum annuum)*
and (below) strawflower *(Helichrysum bracteatum)*

Opposite

VARIETY: Button eryngo *(Eryngium yuccifolium)*

What, When & How to Dry – True Everlastings

Strawflower/everlasting *(Helichrysum bracteatum)*

VARIETY: 'Dragon Fire', 'Purple Red', 'Salmon Rose',
        'Silvery Rose', 'White'

CYCLE: Annual

FLOWERS: Summer to autumn

DRY: Hang upside down

TIP: Cut the central stem when the first flower heads
are open and leave the side shoots to develop for a
second cutting. Pick when the main flower is fully
open. Strip the leaves and leave any buds in place.

Statice *(Limonium sinuatum)*

VARIETY: 'Apricot Beauty', 'Iceberg', 'QIS Lavender',
        'Rose Light'

CYCLE: Annual

FLOWERS: Summer to early autumn

DRY: Hang upside down

TIP: Cut when the florets are fully open and have
begun to turn papery.

Sea lavender/statice *(Limonium latifolium)*

CYCLE: Perennial

FLOWERS: Summer to early autumn

DRY: Hang upside down

TIP: The fluffy yet sturdy flower heads work really
well as a filler for larger displays.

Annual everlasting/common everlasting
(Xeranthemum annuum)

CYCLE: Annual

FLOWERS: Summer

DRY: Hang upside down

TIP: Sow directly into the ground in spring and you
will have flowers within three months.

Globe thistle *(Echinops)*

VARIETY: *E. bannaticus*, *E. ritro* 'Veitch's Blue',
        E. sphaerocephalus 'Arctic Glow'

CYCLE: Perennial

FLOWERS: Summer to early autumn

DRY: Hang upside down

TIP: Best picked before the smaller individual flowers
appear across the entire globe. If picked too late and
left to go over slightly, the head will disintegrate.

Blue eryngo *(Eryngium)*

VARIETY: *E. alpinum* 'Blue Star', *E. bourgatii* 'Picos
        Blue', *E. planum* 'Blue Hobbit', Miss
        Wilmott's Ghost *(Eryngium giganteum)*

CYCLE: Perennial

FLOWERS: Summer to early autumn

DRY: Hang upside down

TIP: Pick and hang to dry just as the tiny individual
flowers burst forth. Eryngiums require cold to break
dormancy and light once sown.

Paper daisy *(Acrolinium)*

VARIETY: 'Double Giant', 'Double mixed'
CYCLE: Annual
FLOWERS: Summer
DRY: Hang upside down

TIP: Can be sown directly or started off in the greenhouse. Prefer poor soil and dry conditions.

Winged everlasting *(Ammobium alatum)*

CYCLE: Annual
FLOWERS: Summer to early autumn
DRY: Hang upside down

Love-lies-bleeding *(Amaranthus caudatus)*

VARIETY: 'Coral Fountain', 'Dreadlocks', 'Viridis'
CYCLE: Annual
FLOWERS: Late summer to autumn
DRY: Hang upside down

TIP: Support the flower heads early when growing by using jute netting to hold them off the ground.

Pink paper daisy/sunray *(Rhodanthe)*

CYCLE: Annual
FLOWERS: Summer
DRY: Hang upside down

TIP: Tricky to grow and prefer full, strong sun and poor, well-drained soil.

Globe amaranth *(Gomphrena globosa)*

VARIETY: 'Fireworks', 'Rose', 'White'
CYCLE: Annual
FLOWERS: Summer to autumn
DRY: Hang upside down

TIP: Enjoys full sun and sometimes flowers through to autumn in a mild year.

Showy amaranth/fox tail *(Amaranthus cruentus)*

VARIETY: 'Hot Biscuits', 'Green Thumb', 'Ooschberg'
CYCLE: Annual
FLOWERS: Late summer to autumn
DRY: Hang upside down

Wheatstraw *(Celosia)*

VARIETY: 'Flamingo Feathers'
CYCLE: Annual
FLOWERS: Summer to early autumn
DRY: Hang upside down

TIP: Easy to start from seed and grow well, withstanding drier summers.

Lonas inodora

CYCLE: Annual
FLOWERS: Summer
DRY: Hang upside down

TIP: Delightful, sunshine-yellow clusters of flowers that dry true to their fresh shades.

For Interest

These are the botanicals that elevate a design, adding points of interest and differing textures, whether that be through their own individual beauty or the way they provide balance and support to other plants in the display.

Many of the plants listed here grow in my borders and line the edges of my parcel of land. I tend to pick them rather sparingly as they aren't prolific flowerers on the whole. Their appearance will change dramatically during the drying phases and may differ each time they are dried – that is, they are less reliable. They have a tendancy to shrink a fair bit too.

Perhaps that's what makes them interesting – they are precious in their scarcity and uniqueness.

Opposite

VARIETY: Marigold *(Calendula officinalis), C. officinalis* 'Sunset Buff' and *Rudbeckia hirta* 'Cherry Brandy'

From Fresh to Dried

Above

VARIETY: Black-eyed Susan *(Rudbeckia hirta)*

Opposite

VARIETY: (Top) Coneflower *(Echinacea purpurea)* and (below)
Zinnia elegans 'Orange King'

What, When & How to Dry – For Interest

Tansy *(Tanacetum vulgare)*

VARIETY: 'Cupid Mix', 'Liliput Series'

CYCLE: Perennial

FLOWERS: Late summer to early autumn

DRY: Hang out to dry

TIP: Pick when the flowers are yellow.

Clary sage *(Salvia sclarea)*

CYCLE: Annual

FLOWERS: Summer to early autumn

DRY: Hang out to dry

TIP: Easy to grow from seed and can be dried once the bracts begin to feel firm to the touch.

False saffron/saffron flower *(Carthamus tinctorius)*

CYCLE: Annual or biennial

FLOWERS: Summer

DRY: Hang upside down

Avens *(Geum)*

VARIETY: 'Mai Tai', 'Pink Petticoats', 'Totally Tangerine'

CYCLE: Perennial

FLOWERS: Late spring to autumn

DRY: Hang upside down

TIP: Both flowers and seedheads are delicate but wonderful dried.

Cardoon *(Cynara cardunculus)*

VARIETY: 'Blood Red', 'Cloth of Gold', 'Sugar Rush'

CYCLE: Perennial

FLOWERS: Summer

DRY: Hang upside down

TIP: Pick when the petals have just begun to fade.

New England aster *(Symphyotrichum novae-angliae)* **and Michaelmas daisy** *(S. novi-belgii)*

VARIETY: 'Composition'

CYCLE: Perennial

FLOWERS: Autumn

DRY: Hang upside down

African marigold *(Tagetes erecta)* **and French marigold** *(T. patula)*

CYCLE: Annual

FLOWERS: Summer to early autumn

DRY: Hang out to dry

Autumn sneezeweed *(Helenium autumnale)*

CYCLE: Perennial

FLOWERS: Summer to early autumn

DRY: Hang upside down

TIP: Stems can be left in situ and picked as needed for interesting structure in winter displays.

Coneflower/black-eyed Susan (Rudbeckia)

VARIETY: *R. hirta* 'Denver Daisy', *R. hirta* 'Sahara
    Goldilocks', *R. occidentalis* 'Green Wizard'
CYCLE: Annual
FLOWERS: Summer to autumn
DRY: Dry upright

TIP: Best dried upright by sticking the stems through
a riddle or something similar that allows them to dry
with their petals open. The structural seedheads
also dry well.

Zinnia elegans

VARIETY: 'Cupid Mix', 'Liliput Series'
CYCLE: Annual
FLOWERS: Late summer to autumn
DRY: Dry upright

TIP: The double varieties are best for drying.

Coneflower (Echinacea)

VARIETY: *E.* 'Cheyenne Spirit', *E.* 'Paradiso Rose',
    E. purpurea and cultivars such as
    'Primadonna Deep Rose'
CYCLE: Perennial
FLOWERS: Summer to early autumn
DRY: Hang upside down or stand upright

TIP: Can be dried when in flower as well as once gone
to seed. Flowers are best dried upright. Seedheads
can be left in situ through autumn.

Cornflower (Centaurea cyanus)

VARIETY: 'Black Ball', 'Classic Fantastic', 'Classic
    Magic', 'Mauve Ball'
CYCLE: Annual
FLOWERS: Summer
DRY: Hang out to dry

TIP: Cut most of the plant and hang as one big stem
when the flowers are still fresh. Petals may be lost
in the process and remain delicate to work with.

Mealy sage (Salvia farinacea)

VARIETY: 'Rose Queen', 'Victoria Blue', 'Victoria White'
CYCLE: Perennial or Annual
FLOWERS: Summer to autumn
DRY: Hang upside down

TIP: Hang out to dry when in full flower or await
the seedheads.

Greater masterwort (Astrantia major)

VARIETY: 'Moulin Rouge', 'Primadonna', 'Rome'
CYCLE: Perennial
FLOWERS: Summer
DRY: Hang upside down or leave in a vase with an
    inch of water until dried out

TIP: Pick when the petals feel papery to the touch.

For Height

As my work has grown and developed, so has my need for the materials I work with to have height in order to create larger installations and immersive designs. In the early days of my journey, I sought out small, delicate, individual blooms to put together flower crowns and wreaths. I've had a lot to learn over the past few years on what can be dried and cut for larger stems. It's important that stems can hold their weight and remain standing for a period of time.

Many of the plants that I use for taller displays can also be broken down to utilise the smaller heads, such as artemisias and *Atriplex* – yet when the entire plant is cut at the base they are something altogether different. *Ammi* left to bleach in the soil and the baking sun of high summer offers statue and grace while *Atriplex* in all its bronze glory creates a stunning, shimmery forest.

Opposite

VARIETY: A display of sunflowers *(Helianthus annuus)*

Flowers Forever

Below

VARIETY: Bishop's flower *(Ammi visnaga)*

Opposite

VARIETY: (Top) *Delphinium consolida* 'Pink Perfection' and (below) *Foeniculum vulgare* 'Purpureum' Bronze Fennel

What, When & How to Dry – For Height

Larkspur *(Delphinium Consolida)*

VARIETY: 'Blue Cloud', 'Lilac', 'Misty Lavender',
        'Smokey Eyes'
CYCLE: Annual
FLOWERS: Summer
DRY: Hang upside down

TIP: Wait until the bottom half of the flowers are in
bloom then cut the entire stem to dry. Self-seeds
easily for stronger plants the following year.

Bergamot/bee balm/horse mint *(Monarda)*

VARIETY: *M.* 'Croftway Pink', *M. didyma* 'Balmy Pink',
        M. didyma 'Balmy Purple'
CYCLE: Perennial
FLOWERS: Summer to early autumn
DRY: Hang upside down

TIP: Can be dried in flower and seed form.

Great burnet *(Sanguisorba officinalis)*

VARIETY: 'Pink Tanna', 'Red Thunder'
CYCLE: Perennial
FLOWERS: Summer to early autumn
DRY: Hang upside down

TIP: Pick when the flowers are still young to ensure
they keep their colour and do not crumble. They will
remain delicate to work with.

Montbretia/copper tips *(Crocosmia)*

VARIETY: 'Hellfire', 'Lucifer', 'Scorchio'
CYCLE: Corm
FLOWERS: Summer to early winter
DRY: Hang upside down

TIP: The flowers dry well and the seedheads can
be left in situ through the autumn and winter to be
picked and used immediately. The leaves can also
be dried.

Purple top *(Verbena bonariensis)*

CYCLE: Perennial
FLOWERS: Summer to early autumn
DRY: Hang upside down

TIP: The petals can fall if picked too soon, so wait
until the flowers are beginning to go to seed. These
flowers retain some purple hues.

Sunflower *(Helianthus annuus)*

VARIETY: Autumn Beauty', 'Claret', 'Earthwalker',
        'Red Sun', 'Ruby Eclipse'
CYCLE: Annual
FLOWERS: Summer to early autumn
DRY: Hang upside down

TIP: Can be dried when in flower but also when the
flowers have gone to seed. Aim to dry just before the
seeds pop.

Giant hyssop *(Agastache)*

VARIETY: 'Blackadder'

CYCLE: Perennial

FLOWERS: Summer to early autumn

DRY: Hang upside down

TIP: Can be dried when in flower with the green foliage as well as once the spires have gone to seed.

Bishop's flower/Queen Anne's lace *(Ammi)*

VARIETY: *A. majus, A. majus* 'Green Mist', *A. visnaga*

CYCLE: Annual

FLOWERS: Summer

DRY: Hang upside down

TIP: Cut the entire plant for height or individual stems for smaller work. The flowers and seedheads dry at all stages of growth. *Ammi majus* can be bleached white when left in full sun or a greenhouse.

Large yellow loosestrife *(Lysimachia punctata)*

VARIETY: *A. majus, A. majus* 'Green Mist', *A. visnaga*

CYCLE: Perennial

FLOWERS: Summer

DRY: Hang upside down

TIP: Can be a bit of a thug but throws out lots of beautiful stems that can be cut right down to the bottom for height.

Bells of Ireland *(Moluccella laevis)*

CYCLE: Annual

FLOWERS: Late summer to early autumn

DRY: Hang upside down

TIP: Pick when all the flowers have developed and opened. If left for lengths of time, the green will soften to a bronze, ideal for winter displays.

Candle larkspur *(Delphinium elatum)*

VARIETY: Black Knight Group, 'Blue Jay', 'Guardian Lavender', Pacific hybrids

CYCLE: Perennial

FLOWERS: Summer

DRY: Hang upside down

TIP: Producing larger flower heads than the annual larkspur, it is best to cut when the top buds are closed and the bottom two thirds are in bloom.

Garden orache *(Atriplex hortensis)*

CYCLE: Hardy annual

FLOWERS: Autumn

DRY: Hang upside down

TIP: Cut tall for height and drying. Break down individual offshoots of seeds for small makes. The seedheads will gradually fade to a petina bronze that shimmers and shines, ideal for winter displays.

From Fresh to Dried

To Fill

Plants that are able to fill spaces and provide a backbone to a design are vitally important to my work. I've learned that I require much more of these than I ever anticipate.

For plants used as fillers, I'm looking for those that maintain their structure and fullness post drying and that can provide a cushioning backdrop to the more focal flowers when used. *The Cloud* on page 201 is a good example of a design in which plenty of filler flowers and foliages have been used. Of course, the reality is that any plant can be used as a filler if you have enough of it, but affordability and availability will need to be considered.

Opposite

VARIETY: *Centaurea cyanus* 'Black Ball'

Above

VARIETY: *Nigella damascena* 'Miss Jekyll's Alba'

Opposite

VARIETY: (Top) *Tanacetum parthenium* 'Flore Pleno' and (below) *Euphorbia amygdaloides* wood spurge

What, When & How to Dry – To Fill

Spurge *(Euphorbia)*

VARIETY: *E. myrsinites*, *E. oblongata*, snow-on-the-
mountains (*E. marginata*), wood spurge
(*E. amygdaloides*)
CYCLE: Perennial
FLOWERS: Summer to autumn
DRY: Hang upside down

TIP: Can be dried both when in flower and once
the flower heads have set seed.

Lady's mantle *(Alchemilla mollis)*

VARIETY: 'Robustica'
CYCLE: Perennial
FLOWERS: Summer to autumn
DRY: Hang upside down

TIP: Cutting in mid-summer will encourage a second
flush of flowers later in the year. The leaves also
dry well.

False goatsbeard *(Astilbe)*

VARIETY: 'Montgomery', 'Spotlight'
CYCLE: Perennial
FLOWERS: Summer for flowers; autumn to early winter
for seedheads
DRY: Hang upside down

TIP: Seedheads can be left in situ and picked as
and when needed throughout autumn.

Wallflower *(Erysimum)*

VARIETY: *E. cheiri* 'Blood Red', *E. cheiri*
'Cloth of Gold', *E.* Sugar Rush Series
CYCLE: Biennial or short-lived perennial
FLOWERS: Spring to early autumn
DRY: Hang upside down

TIP: Both the flowers and the seedheads work
well for drying. Cut at the base and hang out to dry
when at least half the stem is in flower.

Orpine *(Hylotelephium)*

VARIETY: *H.* 'Herbstfreude' and *H. telephium*
Atropurpureum Group 'Purple Emperor'
CYCLE: Perennial
FLOWERS: Summer to autumn
DRY: Hang upside down

TIP: Best picked in autumn when the flower heads
have turned deep red. Can take months to dry.

Feverfew *(Tanacetum parthenium)*

VARIETY: 'Tetra White Wonder'
CYCLE: Perennial
FLOWERS: Summer to early autumn
DRY: Hang out to dry

TIP: The double varieties work best for drying, and
will have a second flush if cut in mid-summer, often
flowering through a mild winter.

Catmint *(Nepeta)*

VARIETY: Dwarf catmint (*N. racemosa*), *N. racemosa*
'Amelia', Siberian catmint (*N. sibirica*)
CYCLE: Perennial
FLOWERS: Late spring to autumn
DRY: Hang upside down

TIP: Cut long stems when flowers have developed.

Flamingo feathers *(Celosia spicata)*

CYCLE: Annual
FLOWERS: Late spring to early autumn
DRY: Dry upright in a vase

TIP: Requires warm, dry summers.

Love-in-a-mist/ragged lady *(Nigella)*

VARIETY: *N. damascena* 'Miss Jekyll Rose',
N. damascena 'Persian Jewels', *N. orientalis*
'Transformer' and *N. papillosa* 'Midnight'
(for the seedheads specifically)
CYCLE: Annual
FLOWERS: Summer to autumn
DRY: Hang upside down

TIP: Flowers and seedheads can be dried. For
seedheads, pick when they are still in-the-green to
avoid seeds spilling when hung out.

Baby's breath *(Gypsophila paniculata)*

VARIETY: *Gypsophila paniculata* 'My Pink'
CYCLE: Annual
FLOWERS: Summer to early autumn
DRY: Dry upright or hang

TIP: Benefits from drying while sat in an inch of water,
which helps to keep the flower heads upright.

Wormwood/mugwort *(Artemisia)*

CYCLE: Perennial
FLOWERS: Late summer to early autumn
DRY: Hang upside down

TIP: Pick once all of the yellow flowers are out.

Yarrow *(Achillea)*

VARIETY: *A. filipendulina* 'Cloth of Gold', *A. millefolium*
'Peggy Sue', *A.* 'Summer Berries',
A. 'Terracotta'
CYCLE: Perennial
FLOWERS: Spring to early autumn
DRY: Hang upside down

TIP: Works well to fill borders with colour throughout
the summer and into autumn. There are some
beautiful soft varieties now as listed above. Pick
when all the flowers are out and the head feels firm
to touch, any earlier and they tend to shrivel and
may lose their colour.

From the Wild

The wild is a precious place and one that we need to take extra-special care of. We must ensure we leave wild spaces as we found them and take nothing more than we need or can sensibly make use of. Many of the plants included here dry well and I now grow them in my garden to avoid taking too many from the wild spaces where they naturally dwell. Some wildflowers and seeds are considered pests and are prolific; others are rare and often protected. Wildflowers and grasses are important sources of food and nectar for our bees, butterflies and other animals. I recommend always checking what the rules are in your local area and forage responsibly. I work according to the principle that if there are very few of a particular flower, I leave them be, but if there is an abundance, then I take just a few and leave the rest. If in doubt, don't take.

For those plants that I discover as being essential for my work (old man's beard, teasels, wild carrot), I will introduce them into my garden to ensure I can access them responsibly.

Opposite

VARIETY: Field forget-me-not *(Myosotis arvensis)*, but not the true wild form

From Fresh to Dried

Above

VARIETY: (Top) Tansy *(Tanacetum vulgare)* and (below) wild carrot *(Daucus carota)*

Opposite

VARIETY: Meadow buttercup *(Ranunculus acris)*

Above

VARIETY: Wild carrot *(Daucus carota)*

Opposite

VARIETY: (Top) Woodland germander *(Teucrium scorodonia)* and (below) red hypericum berries

What, When & How to Dry – From the Wild

Curled/yellow dock *(Rumex crispus)*

CYCLE: Perennial
FLOWERS: Summer
DRY: Hang upside down or upright

TIP: Pick and dry when spires have begun to harden.
Wait too long and they will become brittle.

Common St John's wort *(Hypericum perfoliatum)*

CYCLE: Perennial
FLOWERS: Late autumn to late winter
DRY: Already dried

TIP: Can be discovered in the wild throughout
the late autumn and winter and will already be
dried when picking.

Figwort *(Scrophularia)*

CYCLE: Annual or biennial
FLOWERS: Early autumn to winter
DRY: Hang upside down

Common bistort *(Polygonum bistorta)*

CYCLE: Perennial
FLOWERS: Summer to autumn
DRY: Hang upside down or leave in a vase with
an inch of water until dried out.

Old man's beard/traveller's joy *(Clematis vitalba)*

CYCLE: Perennial
FLOWERS: Early autumn to early winter
DRY: Use immediately

TIP: Pick before the seedheads turn to fluff on
the vine.

Common reed *(Phragmites)*

CYCLE: Perennial
FLOWERS: Late summer to autumn
DRY: Hang upside down

TIP: Pick seedheads early in the season if possible.

Oregano *(Origanum vulgare)*

CYCLE: Perennial
FLOWERS: Summer to early autumn
DRY: Hang upside down

TIP: Break off individual spurs for smaller makes.

Wild carrot/bishop's lace *(Daucus carota)*

CYCLE: Biennial
FLOWERS: Summer to autumn
DRY: Hang upside down

TIP: Both flowers and seedheads can be picked.

Buttercup *(Ranunculus bulbosus)*

CYCLE: Perennial
FLOWERS: Spring to early summer
DRY: Hang out to dry

TIP: Cut long stems when flowers are just opening.

Common knapweed *(Centaurea nigra)*

CYCLE: Annual or perennial
FLOWERS: Summer to late autumn
DRY: Upright in a vase

TIP: At its best in autumn when the flowers have gone over and the silver bases are revealed.

Teasel *(Dipsacus)*

CYCLE: Biennial
FLOWERS: Late autumn to early winter
DRY: Cut when needed

TIP: Seedheads can be cut once they turn brown.

Forget-me-nots *(Myosotis sylvatica)*

CYCLE: Biennial
FLOWERS: Spring
DRY: Hang upside down

TIP: Pick big clumps to hang out to dry. The flowers and stems remain very delicate and so are best worked with as a whole.

Rosebay willow herb *(Chamaenerion angustifolium)*

CYCLE: Perennial
FLOWERS: Early autumn to early winter
DRY: Hang upside down

TIP: Pick earlier in the season.

Goldenrod *(Solidago)*

CYCLE: Perennial
FLOWERS: Summer to autumn
DRY: Upright in a vase

TIP: Dry the flower heads when they have just opened.

Wild chervil/cow parsley *(Anthriscus sylvestris)*

CYCLE: Annual or biennial
FLOWERS: Spring to summer
DRY: Hang upside down

Berries, Grasses & Seedheads

What I love about growing specific plant varieties for their seedheads is that I can enjoy their flowers in situ in the garden or in the growing patch, allowing bees and butterflies to have their fill of nectar and pollen first. I then cut the stems shortly before they burst open to spread their seed, or allow them to overwinter for visual interest.

When drying seedheads the seeds are prone to bursting forth in the process – when this happens I sweep these up and keep them in a box of mixed seed to be sprinkled around the garden the following spring. Some seedheads such as teasels can be left in situ for the winter and picked as and when needed.

Berries, grasses and seedheads are the unsung heroes of the dried flower world. Their shapes, textures and movement can take a display from being staid and lifeless to one of form and flow. There is much to be celebrated within these pages and much more still to be discovered.

Grasses are my new-found love and my appreciation for them continues to grow. Since moving to our new home and leaving the lawn alone for a year to see what grew there, I have discovered just how amazing they can be.

Opposite

VARIETY: Dried seedheads of purple mullein
(Verbascum phoeniceum)

Above

VARIETY: Various naturalised grasses

Opposite

VARIETY: (Top) Seedheads of *Clematis* 'Amazing Kibo' and
(below) the seedpods of a sea of self-seeded love-in-a-mist
(Nigella damascena)

Flowers Forever

Above

VARIETY: Meadow sweet *(Filipendula ulmaria)*

Opposite

VARIETY: Round-headed onion *(Allium sphaerocephalon)*

What, When & How to Dry – Berries, Grasses & Seedheads

Seedheads

Mullein *(Verbascum phoeniceum)*

VARIETY: 'Rosetta', 'Wild Form'
CYCLE: Perennial
FLOWERS: Late summer to early autumn
DRY: Hang upside down

TIP: Structural seedheads for tall displays.

Love-in-the-mist/ragged lady *(Nigella)*

VARIETY: *N. damascena* 'Albion Black Pod',
    A. damascena Miss Jekyll Series,
    N. orientalis 'Transformer'
CYCLE: Hardy annual
FLOWERS: Summer to early autumn
DRY: Hang upside down

TIP: One of the easiest flowers to grow from seed, direct in the soil.

Shoo-fly plant *(Nicandra physalodes)*

CYCLE: Half-hardy annual
FLOWERS: Autumn
DRY: Hang upside down

TIP: Prolific self-seeding plant with seedheads that can be cut on long stems or used individually.

Goat's rue *(Galega)*

CYCLE: Perennial
FLOWERS: Late summer to early autumn
DRY: Hang upside down

TIP: Both the seedpods and flowers can be dried. Cut the stems when the pods are just beginning to form.

Honesty/penny flower *(Lunaria annua)*

VARIETY: 'Chedglow' for purple seedpods
CYCLE: Biannual
FLOWERS: Late spring to summer
DRY: Hang upside down

TIP: Pick the pods when they are still green or mauve. When dry, rub the seedpod between your finger and thumb, and if ready, the outer cases will fall away. I like the seedpods without the outer casing removed and 'Chedglow' is a great variety for purple seedpods that look great in autumn displays.

Poppy *(Papaver)*

VARIETY: Common poppy (*P. rhoeas*), Icelandic poppy
    (*P. nudicaule*), opium poppy (*P. somniferum*),
    Oriental poppy (*P. orientale*), *P. somniferum*
    'Hen and Chickens'
CYCLE: Annual
FLOWERS: Summer to early autumn
DRY: Hang upside down

TIP: One of the easiest flowers to grow from seed, direct in the soil, and will flower profusely. Cut the green before the seedpods turn brown.

Bulbs

VARIETY: Bluebells (*Hyacinthoides non-scripta*),
snake's head fritillary (*Fritillaria meleagris*),
tulip (*Tulipa*)
CYCLE: Bulbs
FLOWERS: Spring
DRY: Hang upside down

Scabious (*Scabiosa*)

VARIETY: Starflower scabious (*S. stellata*) and sweet
scabious (*S. atropurpurea*)
CYCLE: Hardy annual
FLOWERS: Summer to early autumn
DRY: Dry upright

Snapdragon (*Antirrhinum majus*)

VARIETY: 'Black Prince', 'Liberty Lavender'
CYCLE: Hardy annual
FLOWERS: Spring to early autumn
DRY: Hang upside down

TIP: Can be dried both in flower and when they
have gone to seed. When drying the flowers,
dry quickly and at a relatively high heat.

Garden cress (*Lepidium sativum*)

VARIETY: *L. setatum* 'Emerld Beads'
CYCLE: Annual
FLOWERS: Summer to early autumn
DRY: Hang upside down

TIP: A versatile filler that remains green and offers
soft, tiny seedheads in the summer.

Sweet rocket/damask flower (*Hesperis matronalis*)

CYCLE: Perennial
FLOWERS: Spring to late summer
DRY: Hang upside down

TIP: Pick before the plants begin to soften to brown
for stems of long, green seedpods.

Flax (*Linum usitatissimum*)

CYCLE: Hardy annual
FLOWERS: Late summer to early autumn
DRY: Hang upside down

TIP: Cut when turning golden.

Ornamental onion (*Allium*)

VARIETY: A. 'Forelock', round-headed onion
(*A. sphaerocephalon*)
CYCLE: Bulbs
FLOWERS: Late spring to early summer
DRY: Hang upside down

TIP: Pick when flower heads have gone to seed.

Hops (*Humulus lupulus*)

CYCLE: Perennial
FLOWERS: Late summer to winter
DRY: Hang upside down

TIP: Great for making wreath bases and other
structures and the flowers can be used as a filler.
Can also be used fresh and allowed to dry in situ
– be warned they do drop.

What, When & How to Dry – Berries, Grasses & Seedheads

Lupin *(Lupinus polyphyllus)*

CYCLE: Perennial
FLOWERS: Summer
DRY: Hang upside down

TIP: Cut the main shoot once the plant has flowered to encourage shorter stems to flower and set seed.

Foxglove *(Digitalis)*

CYCLE: Perennial
FLOWERS: Summer to early autumn
DRY: Dry upright

TIP: Pick when the seedheads are still green for tall, statuesque stems. Be sure to leave some seeds to encourage flowers the next year.

Field penny-cress *(Thlaspi arvense)*

CYCLE: Annual
FLOWERS: Summer to early autumn
DRY: Dry upright

TIP: Dries to a wonderful soft green. A must have in bouquets and wreaths.

Rhododendron

CYCLE: Shrub
FLOWERS: Early autumn to early winter
DRY: Cut when needed

TIP: Pick straight from the bush once hardened.

Evening primrose *(Oenothera biennis)*

CYCLE: Biennial
FLOWERS: Autumn to early winter
DRY: Hang upside down

TIP: Leave some seedpods in situ to encourage them to set seed and come back the following year.

Coriander *(Coriandrum sativum)*

CYCLE: Annual
FLOWERS: Late summer to early autumn
DRY: Hang upside down

TIP: Pick when the seedpods have developed and are still in the green. They will retain their colour well.

Meadowsweet/meadwort *(Filipendula ulmaria)*

CYCLE: Perennial
FLOWERS: Summer to autumn
DRY: Hang out to dry

TIP: Pick in flower or when gone to seed with both providing great fillers for displays.

Candelabra primrose *(Primula helodoxa)*

CYCLE: Perennial
FLOWERS: Autumn to early winter
DRY: Hang upside down

TIP: Pick throughout autumn before they turn brown.

Berries

Rosehips

CYCLE: Shrub
FLOWERS: Autumn
DRY: Hang upside down

TIP: The smaller the rosehips, the better. Pick when all have turned a flushed red. Expect some wrinkling of the flesh as they dry.

Stinking iris/roast beef plant *(Iris foetidissima)*

CYCLE: Perennial
FLOWERS: Autumn to early winter
DRY: Hang upside down

TIP: Cut when the pods have just burst open for bright orange beauty in displays. The berries should remain safely in their casing.

Grasses – Spreaders

Greater quaking grass *(Briza maxima)*

CYCLE: Annual
FLOWERS: Late spring to summer
DRY: Hang upside down

TIP: Works well in bouquets where the sweet, nodding flower heads add movement and grace.

Common quaking grass/doddering dillies *(Briza media)*

CYCLE: Perennial
FLOWERS: Late spring to summer
DRY: Hang upside down

TIP: A sweeter more delicate relative to greater quaking grass and fully hardy, sometimes leaving some foliage throughout the winter.

What, When & How to Dry – Berries, Grasses & Seedheads

Canary grass *(Phalaris canariensis)*

CYCLE: Annual

FLOWERS: Late spring to summer

DRY: Hang upside down

TIP: Cut before the grass heads soften and brown.

Spangle grass *(Chasmanthium latifolium)*

CYCLE: Perennial

FLOWERS: Late spring to summer

DRY: Hang upside down

Bunnies' tails/hare's tail grass *(Lagurus ovatus)*

CYCLE: Annual

FLOWERS: Late spring to summer

DRY: Hang upside down

Clump-Forming Grasses

Pampas grass *(Cortaderia selloana)*

CYCLE: Perennial

FLOWERS: Autumn

DRY: Hang out or stand to dry

TIP: The large seedheads can be broken down into smaller pieces. Take care of shedding seeds.

Chinese silver grass/eulalia *(Miscanthus sinensis)*

VARIETY: 'Brazil', 'Starlight'

CYCLE: Perennial

FLOWERS: Late spring to summer

DRY: Hang upside down

Fountain grass *(Pennisetum)*

VARIETY: *P. alopecuroides* 'Little Bunny', *P. alopecuroides* 'Red Head', *P. thunbergii* 'Red Buttons'

CYCLE: Perennial

FLOWERS: Late spring to summer

DRY: Hang upside down

Siberian melic *(Melica altissima)*

CYCLE: Perennial

FLOWERS: Late spring to summer

DRY: Hang upside down

TIP: Grows well in a shady spot.

Foxtail millet *(Setaria italica)*

CYCLE: Annual

FLOWERS: Summer to early autumn

DRY: Hang upside down

Wild Grasses

Cat's tail grass/Timothy grass *(Phleum pratense)*

CYCLE: Perennial

FLOWERS: Summer to early autumn

DRY: Hang out or stand to dry

TIP: Pick when still green, so the grass retains most of its colour.

Cock's foot grass *(Dactylis glomerata)*

CYCLE: Perennial

FLOWERS: Summer to early autumn

DRY: Hang upside down

TIP: Retains its shape and structure well throughout the season, so can be picked quite late.

Dart grass/Yorkshire fog *(Holcus lanatus)*

CYCLE: Perennial

FLOWERS: Summer to early autumn

DRY: Hang out or stand to dry

False & poverty oat grass *(Arrhenatherum elatius)*

CYCLE: Perennial

FLOWERS: Summer to early autumn

DRY: Hang upside down

Brown top/common bent *(Agrostis capillaris)*

CYCLE: Perennial

FLOWERS: Summer to early autumn

DRY: Hang upside down

TIP: Can cut clumps straight from the lawn.

Shrubs & Foliage

In late summer, as the long days slip away and autumn begins to arrive, the leaves on the trees begin to turn leathery and are perfect for picking and drying. I collect bundles of leaves at this time of year for use through the winter and early spring. When there is little to be found outside, these saved treasures are much needed.

I usually dry leaves between sheets of cardboard and tissue paper to stop them curling, or hang huge branches in the garage to curl naturally. It's also possible to treat most of the shrubs and foliage included here with glycerine before drying to prolong their useful life and keep them looking glossy. I prefer not to do this – aside from the extra effort, I truly prefer them in their natural, shrunken, crinkly state – but if this appeals to you, follow the steps below to treat and preserve foliage with a glycerine solution. Do keep in mind that treating plants in this way can dramatically change their colour.

1. Gather your chosen shrubs or foliage, ensuring each stem has a clean cut along the bottom and the leaves are undamaged.

2. Fill a vase to no more than 5–7.5 cm (2–3 in) full with a mixture of one part glycerine to two parts water. Sit the stems in the vase and allow the plant material to draw up the glycerine through the stalks (you will probably be able to see this happening) until fully absorbed.

3. Hang up to dry. Note that leaves treated with glycerine will often ooze liquid.

Opposite

VARIETY: *Ginkgo biloba* leaves, pressed and dried

Above

VARIETY: Common heather *(Calluna vulgaris)*

Opposite

VARIETY: Garden asparagus *(Asparagus officinalis)*

Overleaf

VARIETY: Cotinus smoke bush

Flowers Forever

What, When & How to Dry – Shrubs & Foliage

Mountain gum *(Eucalyptus)*

VARIETY: *E. cinerea, E. nicholii, E. pulverulenta*
        'Baby Blue'
CYCLE: Tree or shrub
FLOWERS: All year except when new growth is forming
DRY: Hang upside down

TIP: The leaves need to be picked when they have
aged slightly to ensure they remain green in colour.

Broom *(Genista)*

CYCLE: Tree or shrub
FLOWERS: Early autumn to winter
DRY: Hang upside down

TIP: Pick and dry branches of the stems when
still green.

Hydrangea

CYCLE: Shrub
FLOWERS: Autumn
DRY: Sit upright in an inch of water

TIP: Wait to pick until blooms have begun to toughen,
in much the same way as the leaves on trees do in
autumn. Give the flower heads a feel and if they are
beginning to feel lighter and papery to touch, then
they're ready to pick. Stand the stems upright. The
flower heads won't dry on the bush as the petals
tend to deteriorate, lose their colour and structure.

Barrenwort/bishop's hat *(Epimedium)*

CYCLE: Evergreen perennial
FLOWERS: Autumn to early winter
DRY: Hang upside down or lay flat betwen sheets
    of cardboard

TIP: Can be left on the plant to be picked in the
depths of winter offering a range of hues and
retaining colour well.

Catkins

VARIETY: Hazel *(Corylus avellana)*, silver birch
       (Betula pendula)
CYCLE: Trees or shrub
FLOWERS: Spring
DRY: Cut and stand upright

Tracheophyta

CYCLE: Ferns
FLOWERS: Autumn to winter
DRY: Hang upside down or lay flat between sheets
    of cardboard

TIP: Picking time is of the upmost importance.
Pick too early and the stems and fronds will shrivel.
Pick too late and they become too delicate to work
with. Some ferns can be left throughout autumn and
picked as and when needed once they've turned a
bronze-brown. They can be used straight away or
laid in between sheets of cardboard to flatten.

Plantain lily *(Hosta)*

CYCLE: Perennial
FLOWERS: Late summer to early autumn
DRY: Hang upside down

TIP: Cut the leaves before the plants turn to mush
during a wet autumn. Leaves will curl as they dry.

Copper beech *(Fagus sylvatica* Atropurpurea Group)

CYCLE: Tree
FLOWERS: Early autumn to early winter
DRY: Hang upside down or lay flat between sheets
     of cardboard

TIP: Retains colour well when picked in autumn.
Snip leaves directly from the plant and work with
them immediately.

Mimosa/thorn tree *(Acacia)*

CYCLE: Tree
FLOWERS: Spring for flowers and year round
         for foliage
DRY: Hang upside down

TIP: Can be cut and dried when in flower. Struggles
in harsh winters so needs a sheltered spot to grow.

Garden asparagus/sparrow fern
(Asparagus officinalis)

CYCLE: Bulbs
FLOWERS: Summer
DRY: Cut and stand upright

TIP: Pick and dry while still green when the fronds
and froth have burst forth or leave to turn a bronze
hue later in the season.

Peony *(Paeonia)*

CYCLE: Tuber
FLOWERS: Late summer to early autumn
DRY: Hang upside down

TIP: The leaves retain their colour if picked when
still green. They will curl as they dry.

Maple *(Acer)*

CYCLE: Tree
FLOWERS: Autumn
DRY: Lay flat between sheets of cardboard

TIP: Picking time is important and takes some
practice to get right. Test out leaves by seeing
how easily they break from the branch.

Bracken *(Pteridium aquilinum)*

CYCLE: Ferns
FLOWERS: Autumn
DRY: Lay flat between sheets of cardboard

TIP: Found in absolute abundance in woodland
areas in autumn, bracken is a must-have in any
autumnal display. It will become brittle as time
goes on, so best to use the year that it's picked.

What, When & How to Dry – Shrubs & Foliage

Lavender *(Lavandula)*

CYCLE: Shrubs
FLOWERS: Summer
DRY: Cut and stand upright

TIP: Retaining a beautiful scent, use sparingly
to bring a flash of colour and fragrance to creations.

Orange ball tree *(Buddleja globosa)*

CYCLE: Shrub
FLOWERS: Summer
DRY: Hang upside down

TIP: Dry both the flowers and the seedheads.

Jerusalem sage *(Phlomis fruticosa)*

CYCLE: Shrub
FLOWERS: Late summer to autumn
DRY: Hang upside down

TIP: Pick while still green or allow to go to seed
before picking and using straight from the plant in
autumn. Leave some for ladybirds to overwinter in.

Smoke bush/smoke tree *(Cotinus coggygria)*

CYCLE: Shrubs
FLOWERS: Late summer to early autumn
DRY: Cut and stand upright

TIP: Can be used for largescale work as well as
broken down for smaller pieces. If the seedheads
are picked too early, they tend to shrivel, so be
patient and wait until late summer or early autumn
to pluck them from the bush.

Ivy *(Hedera)*

CYCLE: Evergreen climber
FLOWERS: Autumn to late winter
DRY: Can be used fresh or hung out to dry

Olive *(Olea europaea)*

CYCLE: Tree
FLOWERS: Year round
DRY: Hang upside down

Common heather *(Calluna vulgaris)*

CYCLE: Shrub
FLOWERS: Late summer to autumn
DRY: Hang upside down

TIP: Pick stems early to avoid the petals dropping or
in late autumn when flowers have turned golden.

Coronilla valentina *(Glauca 'Citrina')*

CYCLE: Shrub
FLOWERS: Spring
DRY: Hang upside down

TIP: A rare, spring flower that has a sweet scent.
Cut whole stems for length.

Lily-of-the-valley bush *(Pieris japonica)*

CYCLE: Evergreen shrub

FLOWERS: Spring

DRY: Hang upside down

TIP: Pick when the flowers are fully developed.

Japanse cherry *(Prunus serrulata)*

VARIETY: Prunus 'Kanzan' double cherry blossom,
Kerria japonica

CYCLE: Tree

FLOWERS: Spring

DRY: Hang upside down

Cotton lavender *(Santolina chamaecyperus)*

CYCLE: Evergreen shrub

FLOWERS: Summer

DRY: Hang upside down

TIP: While the flowers, which are teeny and yellow,
dry beautifully, the best part is the foliage, which
is a soft silvery colour, perfect for winter displays.

Russian sage *(Perovskia atriplicifolia)*

CYCLE: Shrub

FLOWERS: Late summer

DRY: Hang upside down

TIP: Cut back hard in late spring for strong growth
the same year. Retains some of its scent when dried.
Dries to a pale purple.

Tricky Folk

All the flowers I reference here are temperamental to work with and more challenging to dry. Unlike a strawflower or statice, it's unlikely that they bring longevity to displays and may lose their colour as well as experience drooping stems and falling petals. While I don't do this myself, flower heads can be wired through the stem to avoid drooping, if required, taking care to maintain the natural shape and flow.

As a general rule, double varieties and darker colours tend to dry the best. Single-petalled varieties and pale colours can be a challenge due to falling petals and colours browning.

All these flowers are very susceptible to damp, and so wherever they are stored or on display must be as dry as possible. Aim for high heat and low to no humidity to encourage them to dry out quickly. Because of how lush and dense these blooms are, the main infliction they will incur is mould. The mould, if it sets in, will usually start in the centre of the flower and spread outwards, resulting in the head falling off the stem. For this reason, the space in which these blooms are dried is incredibly important.

Despite their trickiness, I find these blooms some of the most interesting to work with. They offer the most unique painterly pallette to work with – see *Colour Play* on page 164.

Opposite

VARIETY: Various tulips and ranunculus hanging out to dry

Above

VARIETY: Sweetpeas *(Lathyrus odoratus)*

Opposite

VARIETY: (Top) *Ranunculus* 'Picotee Café au Lait',
cut and conditioned, and (below) *Tulipa* 'Copper Image'

Below

VARIETY: Various Waterlily and Semi-Cactus dahlias

Opposite

VARIETY: (Top) *Tulipa* 'Queen of Night' and (below) *Paeonia latiflora* 'Karl Rosenfield'

What, When & How to Dry – Tricky Folk

Tulip *(Tulipa)*

VARIETY: *T.* 'Brownie', *T.* 'La Belle Epoque',
         T. 'Nachtwacht', wild tulip (*T. sylvestris*)
CYCLE: Bulb
FLOWERS: Spring
DRY: Hang upside down

TIP: Hang flowers individually in the usual way and in an environment that is warm and very dry. They are best dried just as they have fully bloomed.

Buttercup *(Ranunculus)*

VARIETY: *R.* 'Picotee', *R.* Pon-Pon Series
CYCLE: Corm
FLOWERS: Spring to summer
DRY: Hang upside down

TIP: Pick just before the petals begin to fall and stems begin to droop. Single-stemmed varieties don't dry as well.

Dahlia

VARIETY: 'Burlesca', 'Caitlin's Joy', 'Cornel Brons',
         'Gipsy Night', 'Sylvia, 'Wizard of Oz'
CYCLE: Tuber
FLOWERS: Summer to autumn
DRY: Hang upside down

TIP: Strip all the leaves from the stems and hang individually to dry. Dahlias are serious cut-and-come-again plants, so the more the flowers are picked, the more they grow.

Snake's head fritillary *(Fritillaria meleagris)*

CYCLE: Bulbs
FLOWERS: Spring
DRY: Dry upright in a vase in an inch of water

TIP: I pick these sparingly as I prefer them growing in my lawn. Left to dry in a vase of shallow water, they are quite magical in their decay. Very delicate and hard to work with, they are best admired on their own. The seedheads are beautiful when dried.

Peony *(Paeonia)*

VARIETY: *P.* 'Coral Charm', *P. lactiflora* 'Shirley Temple'
CYCLE: Tuber
FLOWERS: Spring to summer
DRY: Hang upside down

TIP: Leaves dry well, so leave in situ if drying the flowers. Pick blooms when open for a few days.

Sweet pea *(Lathyrus odoratus)*

CYCLE: Annual
FLOWERS: Summer to early autumn
DRY: Hang upside down

TIP: Dry both the flowers and the fresh seedpods. Since the flowers are fleshy and delicate, they should be dried quickly and kept in a place free of moisture.

Chrysanths/mums *(Chrysanthemum)*

VARIETY: 'Blenda Purple', 'Bruno Bronze',
        'Smokey Purple'
CYCLE: Annual
FLOWERS: Late summer to autumn
DRY: Hang upside down

TIP: Require hard and fast drying.

Rose *(Rosa)*

CYCLE: Shrub or climber
FLOWERS: Summer to autumn
DRY: Hang upside down

TIP: Roses require warmth and particularly dry
conditions in order to dry well. Smaller, spray roses
are the easiest to dry.

Icelandic poppy *(Papaver nudicaule)*

CYCLE: Perennial
FLOWERS: Summer
DRY: Dry upright in a vase in an inch of water

TIP: Cut stems and leave to fade away in tall
vintage vessels.

Hoary stocks *(Matthiola incana)*

CYCLE: Annual
FLOWERS: Summer to early autumn
DRY: Hang upside down

TIP: Cut when the top buds are still shut and keep
an eye on the stems when drying to ensure they
don't mould. There is a perennial stock that also
dries well.

Creating with Dried Flowers

On Colour

The colours that dried flowers offer are softer versions of those we see when flowers are growing or freshly cut. It's almost as if a filter has been applied to our eyes to reveal delicate colours where vibrant ones once dwelled. The dried flower world is much kinder and gentler than the fresh flower world, one where colours are softened, luminous yellows turn golden and lurid pinks diffuse to resemble the colours found in a late winter's sunset.

My preference is firmly rooted in these quietened colours. I can quite honestly say that I prefer most dahlias and tulips when they're dried to when they're fresh. I greatly appreciate the intense colours of fresh tulips following a dark winter, but I love them so much more when they've faded and have turned tissue-paper soft, lit up by the glow from the window behind them. It's the same for dahlias – when fresh they have the wow factor but when dried, their colours shifting to become more delicate and enticing, that's something else.

When working with dried flowers their softened hues must be embraced and understood. In much the same way that a flower's fragrance won't be the same once dried, the colour won't be either.

The natural fading of dried flowers means that the possibilities for colour combining are vast. Much of the material I work with includes varying shade of colours and there are many painterly bronze and silver options to support the brighter colours when they appear.

PINKS AND REDS

Dahlia

Helichrysum bracteatum 'Silvery Rose'

Paper daisy (*Acrolinium*)

Pink paper daisy (*Rhodanthe*)

Ranunculus asiaticus 'Tecolote Pink'

Russian statice (*Psylliostachys
    suworowii*)

Stinking iris (*Iris foetidissima*) berries

BROWNS

*Amaranthus cruentu*s 'Hot Biscuits'

Bracken (*Pteridium aquilinum*)

Buddleja seedheads

Ferns

Flax (*Linum usitatissimum*)

BLUES

Centaurea 'Blue Carpet'

Clary sage (*Salvia sclarea*)

Delphinium consolida 'Blue Spire'

Delphinium Pacific hybrids

Globe thistle (*Echinops*)

Sea holly (*Eryngium*)

YELLOWS

Achillea filipendulina 'Cloth of Gold'

Goldenrod (*Solidago*)

Helichrysum thianschanicum
    'Golden Baby'

Sunflower (*Helianthus annuus*)

Tansy (*Tanacetum vulgare*)

GREENS

Bells of Ireland (*Moluccella laevis*)

Canary grass (*Phalaris canariensis*)

Catmint (*Nepeta*)

Oregano (*Origanum vulgare*)

Wild mint (*Mentha arvensis*)

WHITES

Anaphalis margaritacea

Delphinium consolida 'White King'

Feverfew (*Tanacetum parthenium*)

Helichrysum bracteatum 'White'

Rhodanthe chlorocephala subsp. *rosea*
    'Pierrot'

Winged everlasting (*Ammobium alatum*)

METALLICS AND PURPLES

Annual everlasting (*Xeranthemum
    annuum*)

Common knapweed (*Centaurea nigra*)
    seedheads

Delphinium consolida 'Smokey Eyes'

Helichrysum bracteatum 'Silvery Rose'

Miss Willmott's ghost (*Eryngium
    giganteum*)

Above

VARIETY: Various *Helicrysum bracteatum*

Opposite

VARIETY: (Top) Dried *Tulipa* 'Copper Image', T. 'Negrita'
and double purple T. and (below) Dried *Tulipa* 'Copper Image'

On Fragrance

This is one feature of dried flowers that I find many of us can be slightly disappointed with, the expectation being that dried flowers will smell as fragrant as they do fresh. The truth is that dried flowers will not smell the same as they did when fresh – a dried rose will not smell like the garden rose as we know it. That is not to say that dried flowers don't have a fragrance; it's just a different, unique aroma and is often indistinguishable from plant to plant.

It's not unusual for people who visit my studio to comment on the scent that fills it, describing it as being calming and floral but not heady. It is there, at a baseline but not at an overpowering level, and certainly unlike the smell that would fill a fresh flower shop. It's really quite hard to describe. The best I can say is that it's like walking into a spice shop or opening the spice drawer in your larder or cupboard, only sweeter. It's all those individual scents brought together in a perfect marriage of fragrance. If you have enough dried flowers in your home or event space, the smell will fill the air and will last, too. When we left our old house and moved to Devon, my cleaner who went on to clean for the new owners sent me a message shortly after we had left to tell me the house still smelt of my flowers, as if they (and we) were still there!

While dried flowers en masse can impart scent when designing with them, we can also use specific varieties to create a full sensory experience. Many of these varieties can be found in a traditional herb garden and border space.

FLOWERS AND FOLIAGE FOR FRAGRANCE

Bergamot (*Monarda didyma*)

Catmint (*Nepeta*)

Hyssop (*Hyssopus officinalis*)

Lemon balm (*Melissa officinalis*)

Marjoram (*Origanum majorana*)

Meadowsweet (*Filipendula ulmaria*)

Mint (*Mentha*)

Rosemary (Rosmarinus officinalis)

Sage (*Salvia officinalis*)

Wormwood (*Artemisia*)

Lavender (*Lavandula*)

AND THOSE TO AVOID

Unfortunately (and this is also the case with fresh), some flowers smell quite awful when dried. Wafts of scents reminiscent of cat pee are quite off-putting, so do take care when drying and working with the following:

Dandelion (*Taraxacum officinale*)

Garden orache (*Atriplex hortensis*)

Ox-eye daisy (*Leucanthemum vulgare*)

Tansy (*Tanacetum vulgare*), although the smell tends to fade when dried

VARIETY: Lavender *(Lavandula)* at optimum picking time

VARIETY: Sun-bleached bishop's flower *(Ammi)*, great burnet
(Sanguisorba officinalis) and the larkspur, *Delphinium
consolida* 'White King'

On Flow

Achieving 'flow' when working with dried flowers can be challenging. By their nature they can be rigid, making it difficult to replicate those billowing, wild scenes from the garden and fresh flower vase.

What I look for in the materials I use in my designs may come down to the individual flowers or seedheads that I select and what they can bring to an arrangement. Or how I can work with materials en masse to bring shape and movement in a way that ebbs and flows naturally.

I adore texture and this love of texture finds its way into my designs. I am forever seeking out new and different plant material to explore its intricacies. Whether it be a fluffy filler to hide a gap or a tall offshoot to draw the eye to its silhouette, it's these individual stems that can elevate a design, allowing it to define the way it sits in a design. As much as possible I celebrate a stem's natural characteristics; after all, these make it unique. Plants that will help you to achieve flow in your designs are listed below.

SOFTLY SOFTLY

Baby's breath (*Gypsophila*)
Fluffy grasses
Old man's beard (*Clematis vitalba*)
Sea lavender (*Limonium latifolium*)

EN MASSE

Baby's breath (*Gypsophila*)
Bracken (*Pteridium aquilinum*)
Mustard seed
Sea lavender (*Limonium latifolium*)

OUT ON A LIMB

Allium seedheads
Coneflower (*Echinacea*) seedheads
Long-stem annual everlasting
(*Xeranthemum annuum*)
Rosebay willow herb (*Chamaenerion angustifolium*) seedheads

FOR ULTIMATE FLOW

Clematis vines
Garden asparagus (*Asparagus officinalis*) seedheads
Love-lies-bleeding (*Amaranthus caudatus*)

Sourcing Your Blooms

Even if you are growing flowers yourself, there may be times when you have to source fresh or dried materials from elsewhere. I always encourage people to source flowers locally where possible, and at the very least from within the country you live. The slow flower movement is gaining traction in many countries and dried flowers are a big part of this, allowing commercial flower growers to extend their growing and selling seasons well beyond the traditional months of the year.

Why Local?

Much has been written about the environmental impact of the mass-market fresh flower industry and of the carbon footprint of flowers grown in heated glasshouses or flown over from other countries. These statistics are compared with those of a flower that is grown close to home using organic and natural methods. When we start to think about the processes and the energy that goes into mass-producing flowers, often year round and out of season, we can begin to understand their impact on the environment and why it's better to buy local.

When it comes to drying flowers, your local grower will most likely be drying in much the same way as I recommend, which is air-drying over a period of a good few weeks at an ambient temperature. When flowers are dried en masse by large businesses, they will often be dried at high temperatures in huge 'flower ovens', using vast amounts of energy, which further adds to their carbon footprint. For this reason, when I'm unable to grow a specific flower for a planned design, I always try to buy fresh local flowers and dry them myself or find a locally-based wholesale provider.

We also need to consider the packaging when buying flowers. I am often aghast at the material that accompanies purchases from flower wholesalers, such as single-use plastic and elastic bands that are unnecessary and difficult to recycle. When buying from your local flower grower, you can always request no plastic and even take your own paper to use as wrapping if necessary.

This may sound a little overwhelming. There are occasions when I have to buy from suppliers further afield, and you may too. I am a firm believer that we should be doing what we can when we can and constantly striving to buy – and do – better. So, when it comes to responsibly sourcing blooms, it is important to do the research, know who you are buying from and what their practices are – and where possible buy local.

Availability

The availability of flowers and foliage for drying has grown exponentially over the past few years. When I first started working with dried materials, I had to buy in much of what I worked with, before I began to grow my own, and it took great effort to find what I needed. Thankfully things are changing at quite a fast pace.

The slow flower movement has been going from strength to strength over the past ten years across most markets as consumer demand catches up with growers and their produce, and dried flowers are much more readily available to purchase. During the COVID-19 pandemic, flower growers found themselves with an excess of flowers as florists were unable to source flowers from abroad. The growers pivoted their businesses to allow them to harvest and dry most of their stock so they could sell it later in the year as single bunches or bouquets. This has made finding locally grown dried flowers much easier, with a bigger, more enticing array of options available.

Finding Your Flowers

Sourcing flowers locally does require a little bit of extra effort, but is well worth it. In the UK we have a very useful organisation called Flowers from the Farm (www.flowersfromthefarm.co.uk), which is a directory of many small-scale flower farmers and florists, and is a great place to start. (You will find resources for other countries on page 220).

The benefit of knowing your local grower is that you can ask questions about their growing and drying processes. If you simply can't find what you are looking for locally or perhaps you need to buy on a slightly larger scale and wholesalers are the only option, then keep an eye out for those websites that specifically list their flowers as being grown locally. Increasingly, responsible sellers are highlighting provenance so you can be sure of your flower's origins.

The Beauty of Home-Grown Blooms

Another important reason to buy your flowers as locally as possible is their appearance and personality. A locally grown and dried flower will have ten times the personality of a mass-produced version. It will twist and turn in each and every way, with colours and hues giving a variety and depth that a uniform, mass-grown flower simply can't. From our flowers to our vegetables, we're led to believe that perfection is best, and that straight carrots and uniform roses rule over imperfections and flaws. I have to disagree. My feeling is that these individualities should be celebrated as they add variety and interest to my garden and my work, and can do the same to yours too.

Creating with Dried Flowers

Leave No Trace

Working with dried flowers is a slow process. It can take up to a year to sow, grow, harvest, dry and turn the resulting dried flowers into a design, which means my work cannot be rushed. I've learned to take a pause in any creative work during the busy months of spring when sowing and preparing the land takes over, to ensure that I am well prepared for the growing and harvesting seasons. If my reserves of dried flowers are low after a busy autumn and winter, then I must wait until I can build those reserves back up, and that takes time.

With all of my work, whether that be a wreath or a larger installation, I try as much as possible to minimise any waste while attempting to keep the materials I use in my designs as natural as possible. On the following pages I share my biggest discoveries over the past few years when it comes to working and creating with dried flowers with as little environmental impact as possible.

Always Look Ahead

Planning is key. I have worked hard at improving the way I plan and record my growing schedule. I make notes each month of what's grown well and how long it took from germination to harvesting. I include which plant materials work well for drying as well as their shapes and forms and how best they dry. This helps me know what is worth sowing for the following year and how I could use the material in my work.

I hang flowers in my studio or air-dry them in the house and attach small labels detailing their growth and drying patterns, and then record this information on a spreadsheet once they have dried successfully.

Throughout the course of the year I draw inspiration from gardens I visit, as well as social media, and begin a list of plants that I want to trial from a drying perspective. Seeds for these will be sought out at the beginning of the following year to go into my trials for that year. This is perhaps one of my favourite parts of my work: exploring new flowers and foliage that will add to my repertoire of drying materials.

Quantities

Drying flowers for the most part will cause the flower to shrink as the moisture is drawn out. For some plants the shrinkage is minimal (as is the case for strawflowers) and for others it's bigger (dahlias and tulips). An armful of fresh *Ammi* or gypsophila will be half the size when dried. It's always worth taking this into consideration when you're growing and drying flowers as you will need to be prepared to grow much more than you think you need.

When installing my work in situ, I will always take more materials than I think I will need. This is nothing new and most of us working with dried or fresh flowers do the same. What is worth noting is that with dried materials, unlike with fresh, nothing will go to waste. Any flowers, seedheads or other materials that aren't used are taken back to my studio, hung back up or boxed for later use. It's important that I always overestimate when I'm planning my growing schedule because dried flowers are not something that can easily be found if I've got the quantities wrong.

Taking Down and Reusing

I always ask to take down my designs or installations myself. Much of the material used in installations or for photoshoots can be repurposed rather than discarded, and I'm passionate about getting the absolute most out of what I grow and create. This not only benefits me, giving me the opportunity to breathe new life into old material, but it also benefits those who have commissioned the installation, as they don't have to worry about disposing of the plant material, which in most instances would end up in landfill or the incinerator.

If the stems are too fragile when I take my work apart, then I keep the flower heads to be used another time and anything that's left over gets chipped down and put onto the compost heap to nurture the soil in my garden later in the year.

The Mechanics

Although it's not always possible to build everything I make out of only natural materials that will go on to be composted, I do try where possible to find alternatives to metals and will never use plastic or floral foam. This takes time and can be challenging, but it's important to me that I work with only natural materials as much as possible.

In the instances where I have to use wire for mechanics and holding things in place, I will strip them away once their job is done and keep them stored for reusing at a later date.

IDEAS FOR NATURAL MECHANICS:

1. Replace chicken wire with bundles of sticks, twigs, vines and straw all bunched together to create a biodegradable nest.

2. Consider using sand and frog pins in place of chicken wire to hold delicate stems in place in a vessel.

3. For hoops and wreaths, use natural vines instead of metal or plastic.

4. Avoid glue and other adhesives that contain chemicals or plastic (most standard floral tapes are made with a film of plastic, meaning they are unsuitable for composting). Instead, opt for paper or wax-coated tape.

It's tempting to buy every shape, colour and size of vessel available, but that can be expensive and unnecessary. I love trawling markets and vintage or antique shops for preloved vases and containers. It's possible to build up quite a collection of unique vessels on a small budget. It's also worth seeking out locally produced pottery – a jug or an ice cream sundae dish work just as well as a vase.

The Need for Natural Materials

It would be remiss of me not to highlight the darker side of the world of dried flowers. It seems somehow that, as humans, we are finding it increasingly hard to let nature be and to enjoy it in its natural state without some form of adjustment or control. Dried flowers are sadly no exception to this. As dried flowers have increased in popularity, so too have flowers that have been preserved in some way. Trend-led products such as neon-coloured bunnies' tail grasses regularly feature on social media platforms, and ice-white bleached ferns can be incredibly enticing if you aren't aware of the unnatural and harmful processes they have been through to achieve this look. Many of these products are being sold as natural when really they are far from it. The Cambridge Dictionary defines natural as: 'found in nature and not involving anything made or done by people'. Many of these products have indeed become manmade simply by virtue of the processes that they have been through.

I find it hard to understand the appeal of these products, given they are so far removed from their original natural form. I worry that this desire for natural materials that no longer look natural stems from our collective and continued disconnect from nature and the natural world. Once you are connected with nature and root yourself and your work in the natural world, it becomes easier to see these things for what they are. Ferns should always be a lush green or painterly bronze as they are in the wild and a bleached white version is inherently wrong. Grasses are pale and neutral in colour when dried and those that have been artificially coloured should be avoided at all costs.

While it may be tempting to brighten a display with artificially dyed or bleached florals, I urge you to resist. It is always a better choice to use materials in their natural state. Embrace the wonder of the natural world and say no to these highly processed, damaging products.

With all that said, sometimes it's really quite hard to know when natural materials have been tampered with. One of the best ways to ensure you are always buying quality natural products is to stay close to your suppliers, whether that be your local flower grower or an online wholesaler. Confusingly, the products I list below are often sold under the umbrella of dried flowers alongside naturally dried flowers, making it incredibly hard to decipher what's been tampered with.

Bleaching

Bleached flowers and foliage have become increasingly popular, often appearing in styled photoshoots that depict an eco, boho or 'natural' style. These flowers and foliage are, however, anything but natural, having been through a lengthy process to achieve the end result. The flowers and foliage are first dipped into different bleaches to remove their natural colour. Much in the same way as bleaching human hair can cause it to appear yellow rather than the craved-for blonde, this doesn't quite achieve the desired uniform white appearance and so they are then put through a further treatment to prevent the yellowing of the stems. Next, yet more chemicals are applied to minimise the smell of bleach. Finally, because the stems of the flowers are now at the point of breaking due to the intense processes they have endured, a final treatment is required to strengthen their stems. This process often uses water-soluble plastics, which is why flowers treated in this way can feel almost rubbery to the touch.

It is, of course, worth remembering that these products cannot be composted and will need to be deposited in the refuse bin, meaning they will most likely end up in landfill or a commercial incinerator.

There are natural, subtle ways to change the appearance of flowers, including sun-bleaching your blooms. Last year I successfully bleached delicate, dried umbellifer flowers such as *Ammi* to an antique white colour. The result was nothing like the pure white of an artificially bleached bloom but achieved a gentler, softer appearance, mimicking how the flowers would look after a scorching hot summer.

I got the best results from hanging the material to be dried in my greenhouse at the height of the summer, although the space does need to be free of moisture (so avoid hanging in a greenhouse full of tomato plants!). Another option could be a garden shed with a window in direct sunlight. This method works particularly well with smaller, more delicate blooms that are lighter in colour in their former state.

Sun-bleached blooms look beautiful among dried grasses and larkspur spurs for a truly whimsical display (see *A Table Full of Everlasting Love* on page 171).

Spraying and Glitter Coating

Every Christmas glitter-coated thistles and holly leaves appear in the shops. Glitter is a microplastic that is permanently adhered to the plant material using glue. Both microplastic and adhesives are damaging to the environment and ensure that a once-natural product is impossible to dispose of in any other way than sending it to landfill or the incinerator.

Aside from turning a natural product into something unnatural, spray painting can also impact a person's health due to the chemicals in the paint, and then there's also the (usually non-recyclable) paint can that will need to be disposed of.

Preserving

This can be a bit of a minefield and very misleading. Even now I occasionally get caught out when I am ordering in dried flowers and so I have learned to question the provenance of everything I buy. Preserving flowers can be done naturally using glycerine (see page 91), but most flowers sold commercially have been preserved using chemicals. This will be noticeable in the way they smell and feel.

There is a huge amount of work to be done within the flower industry when it comes to sustainability. The best we can do as participants in that industry is to continue to ask questions about the products we buy, saying no to those that have been tampered with, and where possible buy from local, well-known sources.

Opposite

VARIETY: *Helichrysum bracteatum* 'Silver Pink' and honesty *(Lunaria annua)* seedpods

Dried Flower Designs

Seeking Out Inspiration

I aspire to create magic with the work that I create and the flowers, seedheads, grasses and leaves that I grow. With these materials, I strive to design illusions that surprise and delight. I bring together colour combinations and textures that I have discovered through growing and drying my own materials, and this is why the growing part of my work is so important. A deep understanding of how nature works and flows together as one has inspired me to incorporate natural pairings in my creations.

Since moving to the country, to a place where I feel enveloped by the natural world, I can't help but notice at a deeper level the way nature works together and how plants intertwine so effortlessly with each other in ways unimaginable in a formal garden setting. Undulating hills of foliage and fauna leave me captivated and the dramatic coastline that rests below our hilltop house and all the flowers that flourish in this hostile environment inspire and encourage me.

All the projects I've included in this book focus on the power and beauty of the natural materials I choose to create with. In some of the projects, single flowers or leaves are used in a multitude of combinations and the techniques stretch from the simplest to the more complex. This is intentional. I have made a concerted effort to explore the many different colours and hues that dried flowers offer and to ensure they are natural in their presentation.

For many of the projects I began by first seeking out the locations to display my designs – all of which are within or close to my house – and created around the space I had found. Working this way ensured the materials and shape of the designs complemented their surroundings.

Finding Your Style

Finding your own style and the elements that make your work unique is something that comes with time, practice and personal exploration. Inspiration comes from all sorts of places, and I swear by finding it away from our screens. Much has been said about the positive and negative impacts of the ease with which we are able to access images of others' work. There's a fine line between being influenced by someone and unintentionally replicating their style or work.

My style has evolved immensely over the years I've been working with dried flowers, much of my growth and shifts coming with increasing levels of confidence as well as knowledge and experiments with growing and drying flowers. In the early days my creations were tight, compact and teeny tiny in size. As I gained more experience and my mind wandered, wanting to explore and experiment more, so did my work. Now while my designs span all sorts of spaces and sizes, how I work and the principles I stay true to have remained the same, and this is where my style comes to life.

The Designs

My intention with the projects in this book is not primarily to teach the mechanics or the 'how to' behind a creation (although I do also explain these). Rather, it is to encourage you to explore your surroundings and to create work that reflects and complements them. I seek to inspire and encourage you to discover the breadth of opportunity that working with dried flowers offers, whether that be for your own home or another environment in a way that is unique to you.

While the materials I work with can be used as inspiration, when creating for a particular space I suggest always taking a moment to absorb the surroundings before deciding upon which flowers would be suitable. To this end, I encourage you not to be limited by the words on these pages, but rather inspired by the imagery and effects.

And finally, as with all things in life, practice is the key to everything. It is how we get better at what we do, by learning from our mistakes and by pushing ourselves beyond our own self-imposed limitations and confidence levels. Practice is what will allow your own style and values to solidify, unify and continue to grow the more you explore. Enjoy!

Dried Flower Designs

Spring Branches

Spring is a hard month for me; the shift in gear so soon after the long winter to such intense and passionate growth leaves me feeling breathless and as if I can't keep up. Everywhere I turn new flowers and foliage are bursting forth out of the ground with astonishing speed and branches laden with blossom sag under the weight of their own beauty. This busyness outside marries with the seed-sowing efforts in the greenhouse – there is no time to stop and slow down when spring arrives.

I have so much adoration for spring blooms – the intense and over-whelming beauty of spring bulbs in particular is so uplifting as their appearance heralds the start of the light returning. But it's the blossoms that fascinate me the most, the billowing clouds of frothy pinks and whites that burst forth, preceding the lush green leaves that follow shortly after. Fleeting in their beauty, I am forever fearful of their demise should a strong spring storm or late frost come rolling through to steal them away. It all feels like the most enormous and wonderful feat of effort and strength in the face of adversity, and I have so much respect for the trees and plants that throw out blooms at this time of year.

Spring is, however, one of the most limiting times when it comes to drying materials. By their nature spring blooms are either fleeting beauties, as with blossoms, or lush blooms such as tulips and daffodils. Everything is so fresh that it's near impossible to dry anything and much of what does dry is delicate to work with.

These spring branches are a perfect juxtaposition of old and new; the lichen-covered branches topped with the sweetest of dried flower heads replicate the fleeting beauty of spring blossoms. They can be hung up or stood in a vase, created en masse or used individually.

MATERIALS

Pliers

Florist's wire or tape (I used wire as I like the effect the gold gives to the branches, but tape can be used as well)

Dried seedheads and flowers with longish stems (I used honesty seedpods and both paper daisies and pink paper daisies in varying colours)

Branches with lots of delicate ends (I used the branches of a hornbeam tree)

METHOD

Using pliers, cut lengths of wire a few centimetres long. Carefully lay out your flowers and seedheads, cutting the stems to a few centimetres in length.

Start to wire the flowers individually to the tips of the branches, using the pliers to squeeze the wire together gently and tightly. This will ensure the delicate stems don't slip out (I avoid using glue to affix the flowers as it renders the branches un-compostable). Take care that the stems are not inadvertently cut when you apply pressure with the pliers.

Continue until the branches are covered with the flowers and seedheads, in much the same way as a fresh blossom branch would be. If you are using different materials as I have, ensure there is a good balance between them.

Stand or hang in situ, ideally where the flowers and seedheads can catch the light.

All

VARIETY: Honesty *(Lunaria annua)* seedpods with pink paper
daisy *(Rhodanthe)* and paper daisy *(Acrolinium)*

Flowers on Fabric

This design combines many of the skills I've learned over the last year, such as sewing, pattern play, flatlaying and colour combining. It is inspired by pressed flowers and how I display them – secured to mottled paper and hung on walls – but instead of pressed flowers, I used dried flowers. Dainty dried flowers that I painstakingly stitched to a square of naturally dyed fabric to create something akin to wallpaper, one that has depth, texture and movement and breathes life into a living space.

Through the early spring months of our first year in our new garden, I carefully collected individual stems of flowers such as forget-me-nots, wild campanula and bird's foot trefoil and hung them out to dry. It started as an experiment to explore how these plants would dry, and when I discovered that they all dried well but were ever so tiny in stature, I wanted to find a way to display them that would showcase their delicate beauty. Smaller, more delicate and therefore lighter flowers are the best ones to use for this project as they won't weigh the fabric down, allowing it to hang without any draping and pulling.

I worked with loose vintage cotton that had been naturally dyed with botanical materials. I chose this material because of its light nature and the way it hangs. Material that is too heavy, such as canvas, would be at odds with the flowers and delicate stems. I also preselected the colour combination of the flowers I worked with and went for blues, yellows and greens to complement the space.

I've since gone on to create framed versions of this design, taking individual stems of my favourite flowers, carefully dried and then sewn onto fabric, and hung them on my walls alongside photos and paintings.

Flowers Forever

MATERIALS

Large piece of fabric

Large sheet of cardboard the same size as your piece of fabric

A selection of dried flowers with their stems and leaves, the smaller and lighter
the better – I used forget-me-nots, wild campanula, bird's foot trefoil, ox-eye daisies
and common tufted vetch

Cotton thread in a colour to complement the fabric

Sewing needle

METHOD

Lay the fabric on the floor on top of a piece of cardboard to allow the
colour to stand out.

Begin to lay out the flower and stems on top of the fabric. Laying out
your design before stitching the flowers onto the fabric gives you the
opportunity to shift things around and identify any gaps in the pattern.
The design can be as rigid or free-flowing as you wish.

Carefully sew each flower onto the fabric, securing in a couple of places,
at the top and the bottom and anywhere else where it flops or needs
help staying in situ. I used a simple thread looped around then tied off
with a double knot. Cut the ends of the thread very close to the knot
so they are barely visible.

Opposite

VARIETY: Forget-me-not *(Myosostis sylvatica),* wild campanula
(Campanula poscharskyana), bird's foot trefoil *(Lotus corniculatus),*
ox-eye daisy *(Leucanthemum vulgare)* and tufted common tufted
vetch *(Vicia cracca)*

Flowers Forever

Verdant Wreath

Wreaths remain one of my favourite designs to create and, as one of the first designs I ever created, it seems fitting to feature one here. Working with fresh materials gives us the opportunity to experience the change in form as they dry. Besides the gypsophila, which was grown in my cut flower beds, all the other materials I used here were picked from the banks that surround my garden, which in late summer produce the most beautiful grasses and wildflowers.

I chose floaty grasses, verdant green wildflowers and honesty seedpods in-the-green (the silvery pods lightly tinged with green reflect the woods and trees around my home), all of which were picked fresh on the day of making.

The wreath is intentionally big, bold and beautiful in order to reflect the wide expanse of forest in which it is on display, yet features delicate details to be discovered upon closer inspection, much in the same way as a lone wildflower or delicate fungi flourishes in a vast woodland. As with all my wreaths, this one was made to be completely compostable and will end its life on my compost heap, ready to nurture next year's soil.

It's worth noting that there's a level of experimentation involved when working with fresh plant materials as not all will work well. I usually trial mine beforehand to see how they will dry once in place. Important things to look out for when working with fresh materials are whether the plants droop, whether the stems stay sturdy and whether the plant material is susceptible to mould.

All

VARIETY: Stems of honeysuckle *(Lonicera),* hops *(Humulus lupulus)*, baby's breath *(Gypsophila)*, honesty *(Lunaria annua)* and a selection of wild green flowers

MATERIALS

Long vines, such as honeysuckle or hop vines

Raffia (you can also use compostable string)

A range of fresh plant materials (I used gypsophila, honesty stems, woodland germander nigella flower heads and meadow sweet seedhead grasses from my lawn)

Two picture hooks (optional)

METHOD

Wrap the long lengths of vine around one another to create a circle slightly smaller than the desired size of the final wreath. The foliage and flowers will increase the size of the wreath once it's complete. The vines should hold each other in place but a small length of raffia or string can be used to secure them further.

Build up the vines to create a large wreath base on which to work. Attach a length of raffia to the top of the vine base. Lay bunches of foliage and flowers on top of the base, then work slowly downwards, securing them at regular intervals by winding the raffia around their stalks. I worked with grasses and wildflowers and began to incorporate gypsophila for the last section, which I secured in long flowing stems to give the illusion of the wreath merging with its surroundings.

To complete the circle, tuck a bunch of material under the first layer and secure with raffia or string, tweaking the foliage lying on top to ensure that all sides and edges of the wreath are covered.

Working with any plant material that has a strong and sturdy stem, carefully thread and poke the stems into the base between the existing raffia. I used honesty stems and extra sprigs of gypsophila to build out any areas that were lacking.

Hang in position with a length of raffia attached to the main vine structure. If the wreath needs to be hung in a certain position, use two lengths of raffia positioned at angles to each other and hang from two hooks.

A Summer Meadow

There is a period, between the heady heights of late summer and the turning of the season in autumn, when the world outside our windows begins to soften and fade. The earth and the plants are beginning to naturally dry out as the height of the summer takes its toll. The burned spires of docks pierce through fields of soft, brown, swaying grasses, road verges fill with statuesque umbellifer seedheads, and I find it almost impossible not to forage on every outing I take.

The scene I have created in this display is a magical one, an illusion of sorts. To many it will appear as if the flowers are growing out of the ground, but, of course, they aren't; they are dried blooms positioned in such a way as to create a field of everlasting beauty. The simplest of ideas that is so beautifully effective and unassuming. This is a way of creating a flower meadow when the flowers have gone over, a nod to the height of summer as the days shorten and fade away.

Due to the nature of the flowers and because the stems are sitting in the ground, this would really only work on a dry day and could only withstand a limited amount of time in situ, so long as the rains and dew do not come down too hard. Once they have been enjoyed, the flowers can be lifted and the stems trimmed to be reused in another project.

MATERIALS

A selection of flower heads and seedheads with strong, long, sturdy stems
(I used a range of plants, including strawflowers, wild carrot, *Achillea filipendula*
'Cloth of Gold' and *Ammi* seedheads)

A selection of taller branches, if desired

METHOD

Choose an area that has some interest already – it could be a natural
field, but ideally not a perfectly manicured lawn, as you want the land
to complement the flowers and seedheads. To the side of our house is
a natural growing space, where we leave the grasses and wildflowers
to grow in abundance. The swaying grass heads provided the perfect
setting for the flower stems that I added in swathes among them.

Carefully push the stems of the flowers and seedheads into the ground
a few centimetres down. If the ground is particularly hard, then
consider using a skewer to pierce a hole in the soil first – this will avoid
any stems being broken.

Using a range of heights and shapes or structures, build up the visuals
of the display, replicating nature as much as possible. Consider creating
clusters of flowers and seedheads, leaving spaces to develop naturally
between them.

Embrace negative space, take in the view from up high as well down
low. Imitate wildflower meadows where clusters of the same flowers
burst forth alongside each other.

Flowers Forever

Dried Flower Designs

Flowers Forever

All

VARIETY: Wild carrot *(Daucus carota)* seedheads, *Achillea filipendulina* 'Cloth of Gold' and strawflower *(Helichrysum bracteatum)* in a variety of colours

Colour Play

With this design I really wanted to show the depth of colour that can be achieved when working with dried flowers, and that colour comes from unexpected places such as dahlias and zinnias. I incorporated naturally dyed ribbons to further build upon the gentle, warming hues of the flowers and plump out sections of the creation where needed.

There is a huge misconception that dried flowers can't be colourful in any other way than through the happy faces of strawflowers. But this is simply not the case. It is true that through the natural drying process they can fade and lose some of their vibrancy, and the strength that they hold in the garden slips away. But despite this, colour can still be found. Colour can also be enhanced to give dried flowers a little lift.

Positioned above a window, catching the light as it pours in here, the ribbons and petals are lit up from behind. When creating this design, I left the stems long on the flowers and weaved them throughout the base of the structure to allow me to reuse them once the installation has served its purpose.

Opposite

VARIETY: Coneflower *(Rudbeckia)*, peony *(Paeonia)*, tulip and dahlia flowers, all dried

Dried Flower Designs

MATERIALS

Chicken wire

Wire cutters

Hammer and nails

Dried flower heads on stems, with a mixture of sizes, colours and textures
(I used dahlias, peonies, ranunculus and zinnias)

Lengths of botanically dyed ribbons in varying colours and materials

METHOD

Cut a length of chicken wire to the size and shape you wish to work with, remembering that whatever shape you create will have an impact on the look of the final design. The shape here is very long and thin with tapering ends and kinks and folds.

Scrunch the chicken wire together, ensuring that the sharp ends are tucked in. If positioning the display against a wall, as I have here, flatten the back of the design so that it will sit flush and hang securely from the nails.

Mark where the design will sit on the wall or surface and hammer in a number of nails from which to hang the structure – the structure will remain relatively light, so a few small nails should suffice.

Once the chicken wire is in place, begin to position the flowers by slowly threading and weaving them into the wire. They will hold each other in place as more and more stems are slotted in.

Lay the flowers out in colour order. As natural gaps appear between the flowers, gradually fill them with tied-up ribbons, allowing some ends to float down at different lengths and angles.

Dried Flower Designs

Dried Flower Designs

A Table Full of Everlasting Love

Here in the UK, it's a rare day when the weather is balmy and calm enough to sit outside in the evening under the stars with friends and families. When this does happen, it is that little bit more special and deserves to be celebrated. This tablescape is where I dream of spending time with loved ones as the sun slips away at the end of another day. It's a place to kick back as the days get shorter, casting an ethereal light over everything, a light that softens the edges of life.

When creating a tablescape like this, it's not only the flowers that must be carefully considered – the materials and items you curate are just as important. I used naturally dyed fabrics running along the table in hues that complement the burned grasses the table is sitting on. The vessels are a combination of pottery and glass, new and old. Vintage cutlery and a mismatch of plates and dishes bring the setting together. Every small detail is intentional.

MATERIALS

Naturally dyed fabric for tablecloth

Tall flowers (I used bleached *Ammi* and *Sanguisorba* stems)

A selection of strawflowers

METHOD

The table here is intentionally unlaid. Plates and cutlery are stacked rather than set to invite and avoid formality. Lay yours how you wish.

Choose a number of vessels to run along the middle of the table, all of differing statures and sizes. I worked with small vintage jars alongside larger preloved ceramic vessels and vases.

Fill the larger vessels with tall flowers to give height to the table while allowing eyes to meet across the delicate stems. I used a combination of bleached *Ammi* and tall, twisty *Sanguisorba* stems. To create interest at a lower level, secure together bunches of tightly linked, blousy heads of strawflowers. Still vibrant and inviting in appearance, I sat mine in amber pots that caught the sunlight as it peeked through the clouds. Cut the stems of these clusters short so the heads of the flowers nestle on the rim of the smaller vessels.

Position the vessels along the centre of the table, giving consideration to how they work together.

TIP

Even the slightest breeze can send vases and vessels toppling over, so fill them with dry sand before assembling to ensure they stay upright.

All

VARIETY: Sun-bleached bishop's flower *(Ammi majus)*, great burnet *(Sanguisorba officinalis)* and strawflowers *(Helichrysum bracteatum)*

Flowers Forever

Dried Flower Designs

Creating Drama & Scale

There is nothing particularly special about the garage in which this design dwells, although it was the inspiration for its creation – my desire to show how easily a nondescript space can be transformed.

I started with swathes of naturally dyed fabric hung from the ceilings and walls, to provide the perfect backdrop for dried flowers, grasses, seedheads and twigs all gathered from the hedgerows. The fabric serves to set off rather than take away from the dried flowers' intricacies and allows for some mesmerising shadow play. It works hard to draw the space together, softening harsh edges and lighting shady corners.

I selected grasses and seedheads with interesting textures and structures, such as wild parsnip and poppies, which I placed in gently undulating groupings, mirroring the way clusters grow together naturally in the wild. I focused very much on warm, muted, pared-down tones which, as the design evolved and took shape, became reminiscent of the glowing sun as it sets over the fields adjacent to my house.

I did not attempt to hide the mechanics here. They became part of the design and added to the story I wanted to tell – a juxtaposition of harsh metals and stones with the fine, delicate stems of plants and a nod to the way nature will always prevail over manmade spaces, when allowed the freedom and time to do so.

Opposite

VARIETY: Foxglove *(Digitalis)*, wild parsnip *(Pastinaca sativa)* and poppy *(Papaver)* seedheads, various umbellifers and *Miscanthus* grass

MATERIALS

Naturally dyed fabric

Chicken wire

Stones and pieces of granite

Florist's wire

Dried flowers (I used foxgloves, wild parsnip and poppy seedheads, and wild umbellifers) and grass (I used *Miscanthus*)

METHOD

Attach long lengths of fabric to the walls or ceiling of your space, so they drape down. Secure the corners and edges to one another by tying them together, allowing the fabric to hang in arches. These curves will draw the eye into the display nestled among the fabric.

Fill some bundles of chicken wire with stones and pieces of granite. Lay these bundles in a rough shape on the floor in front of and between the fabric to dictate where the flowers and grass will go.

Using lengths of florist's wire, bundle together multiple stems of the same flower or grass to make larger displays of the same item – for example, bunches of five to eight stems of *miscanthus*.

Position taller stems, such as foxgloves and wild parsnip seedheads, towards the back of the display in clusters of five or more to bring height and stature. Now add tall seedheads on long, sturdy stems, flowing grasses and wild umbellifers to create undulating movement and focus.

Place clumps of wild, fluffy grasses lower down and slotted in between the tall stems.

Dried Flower Designs

Autumn Harvest

Autumn is my favourite season, one of absolute abundance and bounty as armfuls of flowers are harvested for drying. The hard slog of the growing year is done and if all has gone well, the rewards will be reaped in the form of endless flowers to hang out to dry.

Plants are slowly beginning to decay, preparing to put goodness back into the soil for future flowers and seasons. The hues of autumn mirror those of spring in their intensity, with beech leaves curling and bronzing and seedheads and grasses shifting to translucent golds and bronzes. Autumn is a sight to behold and one that I savour until the very last leaf is left hanging on the tree.

This design is inspired by a visual I happened upon in a loved one's barn – a broken ceiling window that had filled with long since dead and decaying leaves and vines that had crept in to cling to any surface they could find. The low light of late summer streamed in through the frosted glass, highlighting the crisp, delicate leaves and the cobwebs floating in between.

To recreate this scene, I used the simplest of materials. Leaves and vines fill the glass space, giving the sense of the outside coming in, and reflecting the turning of the leaves outside and the return of autumn proper. I had saved many different leaves and seedheads in anticipation of this creation, but when it came to it, leaves and vines were all that were needed.

The light is the most crucial element of this design. Without it the leaves look flat and dull. So, the space in which I created the installation was the single most important factor. My front porch was cleverly designed to look out upon the layers of trees and shrubs that fill the front garden. It is atrium-like with floor-to-ceiling glass. This allows light to flood in from all angles and light up the leaves from behind, bringing them to life.

Dried Flower Designs

MATERIALS

Picture hooks plus a hammer and nails

Dried leaves on branches (I used copper beech), pressed between sheets of cardboard to flatten

Hop vines with the heads and leaves intact

Malleable wire

Chicken wire

METHOD

You'll need a wooden window or door frame for this display, so you can nail it in place. Lightly tap the picture hooks into the wooden frame. I attached mine to the windows and door of my porch. Tuck branches of copper beech leaves onto the hooks. Hang hop vines from the hooks to add drape and flow to the display and give the impression of nature creeping in and slowly taking over.

Where necessary, secure individual leaves to lengths of wire and run these from the main display out, up and over the wooden support, giving the illusion of leaves falling from trees.

Leave enough gaps and space for the leaves so they are not over-shadowing each other, in much the same way that leaves grow on trees in a forest. You may wish to create this installation over the course of a number of days so you can explore the way the light falls, adding or taking away material as necessary.

Opposite

VARIETY: Copper beech leaves

Three Ways with Vessels

From the simplest of combinations to the grandest of designs, there are many ways to display everlastings. Here, I will show you three simple ways to bring them into a living space. Much of the visual appeal will come down to the vessel and the plant materials selected should reflect and complement the vessel in which they sit as well as the space within which they will be positioned.

With fresh flowers you have all the faff of them needing water and being concerned about how long they will last before the petals wilt and fall. While we don't have to worry about that with dried flowers there are other challenges, such as how to hold the stems in place. Stems can be too thin, delicate or brittle to be held in situ, or so tough they are impossible to push into a frog pin. So, here are my favourite methods for holding stems in place in jars, vases and other vessels.

SAND

Fill your vessel with soft, dry sand, which will act a little like floral foam and allow more delicate stems to stand upright on their own.

PINE NEEDLES

Gather handfuls of pine needles from the forest floor and place them in your vessel vertically until the entire space is filled. The pine needles provide strength and structure for stems and stop them flopping.

FROG PINS AND CHICKEN WIRE

Frog pins alone can be tricky if you are working with delicate stems and tougher foliage or branches. I often combine a frog pin with chicken wire to hold everything neatly in place. This works particularly well for larger vessels.

Dried Flower Designs

DESIGN 1: *Simplicity*

Since moving to Devon and allowing our grass to grow long to provide habitats and food sources for insects, I have noticed the true breadth of wild grasses that grow here and often use them in my arrangements, complementing them with ornamental grasses such as quaking grass (*Briza*) and canary grass (*Phalaris canadensis*).

Often the simplest way to display grasses is on their own, with a few stems in a vase, to bring texture and shadow to a room.

Place the grasses in vintage vessels in neutral colours and then position them where they will catch the afternoon light.

For wider necked vessels, I suggest placing sand at the bottom to keep the stems upright.

The beauty of this display is the simplicity of the stems, the light in which they sit and the shadows they create.

DESIGN 2: *All the Neutrals*

The starting point for this design was the vase, which I found at my local vintage market. I selected seedheads and lichen-covered branches from my studio to form the base of the display and complemented them with the soft tones of white strawflowers.

To ensure the materials stay upright in the vessel, scrunch up a big ball of chicken wire quite tightly and force it into the opening of the vessel to sit at the bottom.

Create the outline shape of the design – I used lichen-covered branches – before adding the other materials. I worked with a complex mixture of structures and textures, including the fluffy seedheads of clematis vines and the patina'd stems of *Atriplex*. Taut sunflower seedheads, near bursting at the seams, nestled in among it all.

Dried Flower Designs

Flowers Forever

All

VARIETY: Pompom dahlias, fluffy grass heads, shepherd's
purse *(Capsella bursa-pastoris)* and sprigs of artemisia
seedheads and ranunculus

DESIGN 3: *It's All in the Details*

Working with some of the smallest flowers I had dried the previous summer, this design (see pages 196–197) is all about celebrating the little details.

Choose smaller everlastings for this display. I opted for pompom dahlias that dried to be no bigger than a broadbean and nestled them among fluffy grass heads that were cut down to create small, floaty wonders. These are then balanced out with the heart-shaped seedheads of shepherd's purse and sprigs of artemisia.

The heads of the ranunculus are beginning to drop, but I think this helps to soften the rigidity of the other stems that they sit among.

The palette of this floral display is soft and muted, with a touch of dusky pinks and peaches. I love how the design spreads and flowers out of the vessel.

The Cloud

The concept for this installation is not a new one. Hanging flower clouds, as they are commonly known, have become increasingly popular. So often we think of installations as one-time, static objects, but that needn't be the case, particularly when working with dried flowers. I wanted to create an installation that was moveable, to allow it to be hung outside and brought in if the winds picked up and the rain came down.

The Cloud was entirely inspired by the magical peach house in which it hangs. The fluffy skin and plump, juicy flesh of the peaches alongside the heavily laden drooping branches are replicated in the cloud's shape and structure. Lots of delicate blooms and seedheads come together en masse to form a billowing, ballooning cloud in hues that match the skies outside.

Flower clouds are an absolute joy to create and while the mechanics and structure will probably not differ from one to the other, the shape and flow can change dramatically depending upon the materials used and the space in which they sit. It is also important to consider the flow and shape of the cloud by defining the shape and size of the chicken wire base – which should be indicative of the end vision – from the start. These clouds can be built on location or in another space and then transported to the venue.

Opposite

VARIETY: Garden cress *(Lepidium setatum)*, larkspur *(Delphinium consolida)*, thyme *(Thymus)*, statice *(Limonium sinuatum)* and sea lavender *(Limonium latifolium)*

Dried Flower Designs

MATERIALS

Chicken wire

Florist's or garden wire

Hooks

Dried flowers and foliage (I used garden cress, lepimedium, Pastel mixed, limonium safora dark blue, larkspur misty and sea lavender, smoky eyes, flowering thyme and statice)

METHOD

Shape the chicken wire into a form that works for the space you are creating within and one that is reflective of the flow of the end design. If the base structure undulates, so too willl the flower cloud; if the base structure is long and thin, then the flower cloud will also be like this. I tend to scrunch up my chicken wire to ensure there are lots of lengths of wire to hold the stems in place. Bend any loose ends around and inwards to fix them together and ensure no niggling, painful ends of wire are sticking out.

Attach a length of florist's or garden wire to each end of the wire frame and hang from hooks.

Break off lengths of lepidium and gently poke them into the chicken wire to build up a soft base. Working with a combination of flat-headed flowers like statice and sea lavender, position clusters of the flowers together to bring depth and colour. The aim is for each element to flow into the other, giving the impression of a whole made out of many small parts.

I used long-stemmed flowers, including larkspur, to encourage the cloud to flow down and mimic the laden branches of the peach tree it would sit under, filling in any gaps with garden cress and flowering thyme to soften the green. I deliberately avoided using focal flowers for this design, instead wanting to create a visual that appeared to be as one rather than many combined.

Flowers Forever

Winter Solstice

It's taken me a long time to make peace with winter and all that comes with it. The lack of light and seemingly barren land outside would often leave me feeling desolate and melancholy. However, the more I work on the land and spend time outside, no matter what the season, the more I've come to realise that winter is not something to be feared, and rather a season to be appreciated. While the branches may be bare and the ground frozen solid, there is so much going on deep down beneath the surface. Winter is a time for building strength, for giving back to oneself, and nature shows us just how important that is. Although winter is a season of scarcity, it is also one of self-nourishment.

Now I look forward to the winter months, to the quiet, cosy moments spent inside with loved ones and having the time to rest and recoup – the perfect antidote to the hedonistic days of summer. In much the same way that the natural world is hunkering down and replenishing, I have learned to do the same.

To create designs in winter with the materials the season has to offer requires patience and a keen eye. Fresh flowers and foliage are at a bare minimum so the reserves I've built up throughout the year will provide me with much of the material that I need. There's still much beauty to be found outside, though – ferns are at their absolute best in winter, having partly dried on their stems, and do well when picked and pressed. The statuesque seedheads of teasels and other perennials can be plucked from road verges, field margins and the garden, if they have been left to go over.

This design is one of simplicity, of catching and working with the light and noticing the magic. Inspired by frosty mornings and cold, foggy days here in Devon, I borrowed a good friend's potting shed and hung honesty seedpods among the cobwebs and spiders. Winter appeared in the potting shed, in all its sparkling, magical, understated glory.

All

VARIETY: Honesty *(Lunaria annua)*

Flowers Forever

MATERIALS

Chicken wire

Honesty seedheads – peeled and kept on their stems

Thin florist's wire in gold or silver

METHOD

Create the base of the build by hanging a flat length of chicken wire from the ceiling where the design is to be installed.

Secure small bunches of honesty seedheads to a length of florist's wire by twisting the wire around the stems. Aim to add five to six clusters at regular intervals to give the appearance of the flowers hanging along one long branch. This allows for flow and movement; something a long, straight stem of honesty won't give.

Once each length of florist's wire is complete, cut it from the reel. Loop that length of wire through the wire base on the ceiling, gently twisting it to secure it in place. Press kinks and folds in the wire to give the honesty movement.

Continue to build up the design with more lengths of seedheads, considering carefully where they hang – they are at their best when the light shines on them. In this design I trailed them down in front of the window so they caught the late evening light.

Flowers Forever

Flowers Forever

About the Author & Acknowledgements

About

Founder of Botanical Tales and author of *Everlastings*, Bex Partridge is a floral artist specialising in dried flowers whose work is continually inspired by nature, the ebb and flow of the seasons and sustainability.

Alongside making her own dried flower art, Bex runs creative workshops as well as sharing advice and inspiration on both her blog and social media channels.

Acknowledgements

This book was a hard slog, written in the depths of the darkest years of our life so far. With the boys at home and having just moved to a new home, we were deep in lockdown, homeschooling and working, and generally trying to survive as a family. This didn't make things easy and so I am very grateful to those many people who supported me through it. I can't actually believe we made it happen.

To Ed, for trusting me when I told you we needed to follow our hearts and our instincts and move house in the middle of a pandemic. For fitting out the cabin to create my studio the moment we moved in, for putting up my greenhouse in the middle of winter with the tips of your fingers frozen cold, so I could grow flowers for the shoot, and for building the bones of my garden. But above all for being you, kind you. I love you to the moon and back.

To my boys, for being the most beautiful, generous, creative humans. I learn from you every day and your respect for my work makes this so much easier.

To my mum, for putting her teacher's hat back on and marking my work! Thanks for making my sentences make sense and correct!

To everyone in my new community who loaned me props, allowed me to use their spaces and most of all welcomed us with open arms. We had been in Devon for less than a year when I came knocking for favours. Sara and Luke for the loan of the cobwebby, old gardener's shed, now immortalised in these pages. Adam and Lydia for the most magical peach house and Lucy Brazier for the loan of props I struggled to source myself.

To Tracey, Hedgerow and Bloom, for welcoming Laura and I to your flower field the year before I moved. You are such a kind, generous soul and I miss you and your flowers immensely.

The Hardie Grant team for always trusting and believing. Kajal, your leadership and passion for supporting authors is admirable. I am so grateful that I found you and that you continue to see growth and potential in me.

Kate, for pulling it all together and keeping me on the straight and narrow. For remaining calm when timings and locations changed – it's been a pleasure working with you.

And to Clare, for the most sophisticated design I could have dreamed of.

Laura! I am deeply honoured to have worked with you again. You are the most talented photographer. I adored having you here in my space by my side, following me on my bonkers journey to photograph wrecks of cars and scabby sheds. You get me and I feel blessed to call you a friend.

To Matt, thank you for being a calm and wonderful support to us all during the shoots. Tina misses you!

To the sea for being my therapy this past year and to the garden. I pinch myself every day in utter disbelief that I get to call this place home. The green and the mud and the neverending stream of wildlife that crosses our paths. I have never felt more grounded.

Resources

Owen Wormser, *Lawns into Meadows*, Stone Pier Press, 2020

Flowers from the Farm, www.flowersfromthefarm.co.uk
An award-winning membership association championing artisan
growers of seasonal, scented and locally grown British cut flowers

The Land Gardeners, www.thelandgardeners.com
Providing courses and advice on how to make compost

Charles Dowding, www.charlesdowding.co.uk
For advice and courses on no-dig gardening

Piet Oudolf, gardener and author of *Matrix Planting*

Suppliers

Organic Bulbs
    www.organicbulbs.com
Naturally Dyed Fabrics
    The Natural Dyeworks, www.thenaturaldyeworks.com
    Mia Sylvia, www.miasylvia.co.uk
Dried flowers
    Essentially Hops, www.essentiallyhops.co.uk
    Atlas Flowers, www.atlasflowers.co.uk
Snips
    Niwaki, www.niwaki.com
Seed trays
    Container wise, https://containerwise.co.uk
Seeds
    Chiltern Seeds, www.chilternseeds.co.uk
    Green and Gorgeous, www.greenandgorgeousflowers.co.uk
    Grace Alexander, www.gracealexanderflowers.co.uk

Index

Italics are used for projects, botanical names and page refs for illustrations

A

African marigold (*Tagetes erecta*) 56
Albion black pod (*Nigella damascena*) 45
Amazing grey (*Papaver rhoeas*) *35*
Amazing Kibo (*Clematis*) *80*
Annual everlasting (*Xeranthemum Annum*) *48*, 50
annuals 20–1
Autumn Harvest 185–9
Autumn sneezeweed (*Helenium autumnale*) 56
Avens (*Geum*) 56

B

Baby's breath (*Gypsophila paniculata*) 69
   Verdant Wreath 151–5
Barrenwort (*Epimedium*) 96
Bee balm (*Monarda*) 62
Bells of Ireland (*Moluccella laevis*) 63
Bergamot (*Monarda*) 62
berries 79, 87
Bird's foot trefoil (*Lotus corniculatus*) *27*
   Flowers on Fabric 144–9
Bishop's flower (*Ammi visnaga*) 60, 63, *116*
   A Table Full of Everlasting Love 171–5
Bishop's hat (*Epimedium*) 96
Bishop's lace (*Daucus carota*) 73, 75, 77
Black ball (*Centaurea cyanus*) 65
Black-eyed Susan (*Rudbeckia hirta*) *55*, 57
bleaching 128–9
Blue eryngo (*Eryngium*) 50
Bluebells (*Hyacinthoides non-scripta*) 85
Bracken (*Pteridium aquilinum*) 97
Bronze fennel (*Foeniculum vulgare* 'Purpureum') *60*
Broom (*Genista*) 96
Brown top (*Agrostis capillaris*) 89
Bulbs 85
Bunnies' tails (*Lagurus ovatus*) 88

Buttercup (*Ranunculus*) 77, 106
Button eryngo (*Eryngium yuccifolium*) *49*

C

Canary grass (*Phalaris canariensis*) 88
Candelabra primrose (*Primula helodoxa*) 87
Candle larkspur (*Delphinium elatum*) 63
Cardoon (*Cynara cardunculus*) 56
Catkins 96
Catmint (*Nepeta*) 69
Cat's tail grass (*Phleum pratense*) 89
chemical-free gardening 34–7
Cherry brandy (*Rudbeckia hirta*) *53*
Chinese silver grass (*Miscanthus sinensis*) 88
Chrysanths/mums (*Chrysanthemum*) 107
Clary sage (*Salvia sclarea*) 56
Classic magic (*Centaura cyanus*) *19*
Cloth of gold (*Achillea filipendulina*)
   A Summer Meadow 157–63
The Cloud 201–7
Cock's foot grass (*Dactylis glomerata*) 89
colour 42, 110–13
Colour Play 164–9
Common bent (*Agrostis capillaris*) 89
Common bistort (*Polygonum bistorta*) 76
Common everlasting (*Xeranthemum Annum*) 50
Common heather (*Calluna vulgaris*) *93*, 98
Common knapweed (*Centaurea nigra*) 77
Common quaking grass (*Briza media*) 87
Common reed (*Phragmites australis*) 76
Common St John's wort (*Hypericum perfoliatum*) 76
compost 34
Coneflower (*Echinacea*) *55*, 57
   Colour Play 164–9
Copper beech (*Fagus sylvatica Atropurpurea Group*) 97
Copper image (*Tulipa*) *103*
Copper Image (*Tulipa*) *113*
Copper tips (*Crocosmia*) 62, 96
Coriander (*Coriandrum sativum*) 86
Cornflower (*Centaurea cyanus*) 57

Cotinus smoke bush *93*
Cow parsley (*Anthriscus sylvestris*) 77
Creating Drama & Scale 177–83
Curled dock (*Rumex crispus*) *45*, 76

D

Dahlias *12*, *104*, 106
   Colour Play 164–9
Damask flower (*Hesperis matronalis*) 85
Dart grass (*Holcus lanatus*) 89
decay, beauty of 10
designs
   Autumn Harvest 185–9
   The Cloud 201–7
   Colour Play 164–9
   Creating Drama & Scale 177–83
   Flowers on Fabric 144–9
   inspiration for 135–6
   Spring Branches 138–43
   A Summer Meadow 157–63
   A Table Full of Everlasting Love 171–5
   Three Ways with Vessels 191–9
   Verdant Wreath 151–5
   Winter Solstice 209–15
Doddering dillies (*Briza media*) 87
drying process 40–2, 123–4

E

environmental impact 118–21, 123–30
Eulalia (*Miscanthus sinensis*) ·88
Evening primrose (*Oenothera biennis*) 86
Everlasting flower (*Helichrysum bracteatum*) *19*, *48*, 50
   A Summer Meadow 157–63
   A Table Full of Everlasting Love 171–5

F

fabric: *Flowers on Fabric* 144–9

False & poverty oat grass (*Arrhenatherum elatius*) 89

False goatsbeard (*Astilbe*) 68

False saffron (*Carthamus tinctorius*) 56

Feverfew (*Tanacetum parthenium*) 68

Field forget-me-not (*Myosotis arvensis*) 71

Field penny-cress (*Thlaspi arvense*) 86

Figwort (*Scrophularia*) 76

fillers 65–9

Flax (*Linum usitatissimum*) 85

Flore pleno (*Tanacetum parthenium*) 66

flow 117

Flowers on Fabric 144–9

foliage 96–9

Forget-me-nots (*Myosotis sylvatica*) 77

Flowers on Fabric 147

Fountain grass (*Pennisetum*) 88

Fox tail (*Amaranthus cruentus*) 51

Foxglove (*Digitalis*) 86

Creating Drama & Scale 177–83

Foxtail millet (*Setaria italica*) 89

fragrance 114–16

French marigold (*Tagetes patula*) 56

French meadow rue (*Thalictrum aquilegiifolium*) 69

G

Garden asparagus (*Asparagus officinalis*) 93, 97

Garden cress (*Lepidium sativum*) 85

The Cloud 201–7

Garden orache (*Atriplex hortensis*) 86

gardening

benefits of 18

chemical-free 34–7

harvesting water 37

no-dig gardening 33–4

plant protection & support 37

Giant hyssop (*Agastache*) 63

Ginkgo biloba 91

Globe amaranth (*Gomphrena globosa*) 51

Globe thistle (*Echinops*) 50

Goat's rule (*Galega*) 84

Goldenrod (*Solidago*) 77

grasses 79, 87–9

Great burnet (*Sanguisorba officinalis*) 62, 116

A Table Full of Everlasting Love 171–5

Greater masterwort (*Astrantia major*) 57

Greater quaking grass (*Briza maxima*) 87

greenhouses 29

H

Hare's tail grass (*Lagurus ovatus*) 88

harvesting, year-round 25

Heather (*Calluna*) 98

height 58–63

Helichrysum bracteatum 113

Honesty (*Lunaria annua*) 84, *130*

Spring Branches 142–3

Verdant Wreath 151–5

Winter Solstice 209–15

Honeysuckle (*Lonicera*)

Verdant Wreath 151–5

Hops (*Humulus lupulus*) 85

Verdant Wreath 151–5

Horse mint (*Monarda*) 62

Hot biscuits (*Amarantuhus cruentus*) *47*

Hydrangea 41, 96

I

Icelandic poppy (*Papaver nudicaule*) 107

inspiration 135–6

interest & texture 53–7

Ivy (*Hedera*) 98

J

Japanese cherry (*Prunus serrulata*) 99

Jerusalem sage (*Phlomis fruticosa*) 98

K

Karl Rosenfield (*Paeonia latiflora*) *104*

L

Lady's mantle (*Alchemilla mollis*) 68

Larkspur (*Delphinium Consolida*) 62, *116*

The Cloud 201–7

Lavender (*Lavandula*) 98, *115*

lawns 26

light 42

Lily-of-the-valley bush (*Pieris japonica*) 99

local suppliers 118–21

Lonas inadora 51

longevity 14

Love-in-a-mist (*Nigella*) 69, *80*, 84

Love-lies-bleeding (*Amaranthus caudatus*) *47*, 51

Lupin (*Lupinus polyphyllus*) 86

M

Maple (*Acer*) 97

Marigold (*Calendula officinalis*) *53*

Mayweed (*Matricaria discoidea*) *45*

Meadow buttercup (*Ranunculus acris*) *73*

Meadowsweet (*Filipendula ulmaria*) *83*, 86

Meadwort (*Filipendula ulmaria*) *83*, 86

Mealy sage (*Salvia farinacea*) 57

Michaelmas daisy (*Symphyotrichum novi-belgii*) 56

Mimosa (*Acacia*) 97

Miss Jekyll's Alba (*Nigella damascena*) 66

moisture 42

Montbretia (*Crocosmia*) 62, 77

Mountain gum (*Eucalyptus*) 96

Mugwort (*Artemisia*) 69

Mullein (*Verbascum phoeniceum*) 84

N

natural materials 127–30

New England aster (*Symphyotrichum novae-angliae*) 56

no-dig gardening 33–4

O

Old man's beard 76

Olive (*Olea europaea*) 98

Orange ball tree (*Buddleja globosa*) 98

Orange king (*Zinnia elegans*) *55*

Oregano (*Origanum vulgare*) 76

Ornamental onion (*Allium*) 85

Orpine (*Hylotelephium*) 68

Ox-eye daisy (*Leucanthemum vulgare*) *13*

Flowers on Fabric 144–9

P

Pampas grass (*Cortaderia selloana*) 88

Paper daisy (*Acrolinium*) 51

Spring Branches 142–3

peat 34

Penny flower (*Lunaria annua*) 84, *130*

Spring Branches 142–3

Verdant Wreath 151–5

Winter Solstice 209–15

Peony (*Paeonia*) 41, 97, 106

    Colour Play 164–9

perennials *20, 22–3*

picking flowers for drying *41*

Picotee café au lait (*Ranunculus*) *103*

Pink paper daisy (*Rhodanthe*) 51

    Spring Branches 142–3

Pink perfection (*Delphinium consolida*) *60*

planning 123–4

Plantain lily (*Hosta*) 97

plants

    protection & support *37*

    reusing *124–5*

Poppy (*Papaver*) 84

    Creating Drama & Scale 177–83

preserving *130*

projects

    Autumn Harvest 185–9

    The Cloud 201–7

    Colour Play 164–9

    Creating Drama & Scale 177–83

    Flowers on Fabric 144–9

    Spring Branches 138–43

    A Summer Meadow 157–63

    A Table Full of Everlasting Love
        171–5

    Three Ways with Vessels 191–9

    Verdant Wreath 151–5

    Winter Solstice 209–15

protection for plants *37*

Purple mullein (*Verbascum phoeniceum*) *79*

Purple top (*Verbena bonariensis*) *62*

Q

Queen Anne's lace (*Ammi*) *63, 116*

Queen of Night (*Tulipa*) *104*

R

Ragged lady (*Nigella*) 69, *80*, 84

red hypericum berries *75*

reusing plants 124–5

Rhododendron 86

Roast beef plant (*Iris foetidissima*) 87

Rose (*Rosa*) 107

Rosebay willow herb (*Chamaenerion
angustifolium*) 77

Rosehips 87

Round-headed onion (*Allium

sphaerocephalon*) *83*

S

Safflower (*Carthamus tinctorius*) 56

Scabious (*Scabiosa*) 85

Sea lavender (*Limonium latifolium*) 50

    The Cloud 201–7

seedheads 79, 84–7

seeds, collecting 30

Shepherd's purse (*Capsella bursa-pastoris*)

    Three Ways with Vessels 191–9

Shoo-fly plant (*Nicandra physalodes*) 84

Showy amaranth (*Amaranthus cruentus*) 51

shrubs 96–9

Siberian melic (*Melica altissima*) 88

Silver pink (*Helichrysum bracteatum*) *130*

slow flower movement 13, 118, 120

Smoke bush/tree (*Cotinus coggygria*) 98

Snake's head fritillary (*Fritillaria
meleagris*) 85, 106

Snapdragon (*Antirrhinum majus*) 85

sourcing flowers 118–21

Spangle grass (*Chasmanthium latifolium*) 88

Sparrow fern (*Asparagus officinalis*) 93, 97

spraying & glitter coating 129–30

Spring Branches 138–43

Spurge (*Euphorbia*) 68

Statice (*Limonium sinuatum*) 50

    The Cloud 201–7

Stinking iris (*Iris foetidissima*) 87

Strawflower (*Helichrysum bracteatum*)
19, 45, 48, 50, *130*

    A Summer Meadow 157–63

    A Table Full of Everlasting Love
        171–5

structures for support 37

style 135–6

A Summer Meadow 157–63

Sunflower (Helianthus annuus) *58, 62*

Sunray (*Rhodanthe*) 51, *142–3*

sustainability 14

Sweet pea (*Lathyrus odoratus*) *103*, 106

Sweet rocket (*Hesperis matronalis*) 85

T

A Table Full of Everlasting Love 171–5

Tansy (*Tanacetum vulgare*) 56, *73*

Teasel (*Dipsacus*) 77

temperature 42

texture 53–7, 117

Thorn tree (*Acacia*) 97

Three Ways with Vessels 191–9

Timothy grass (*Phleum pratense*) 89

Tracheophyta 96

Traveller's joy (*Clematis vitalba*) 76

tricky plants 100–7

true everlastings 45–51

Tufted hair grass (*Deschampsia cespitosa*) *27*

Tufted vetch (*Vicia cracca*)

    Flowers on Fabric 144–9

Tulip (*Tulipa*) 41, 85, *103*, *104*, 106, *113*

    Colour Play 164–9

V

Verdant Wreath 151–5

W

Wallflower (*Erysimum*) 68

water storage 37

Wheatstraw (*Celosia*) 51

Wild campanula (*Campanula poscharskyana*)

    Flowers on Fabric 144–9

Wild carrot (*Daucus carota*) *73, 75*, 77

    A Summer Meadow 157–63

Wild chervil (*Anthriscus sylvestris*) 77

Wild parsnip (*Pastinaca sativa*)

    Creating Drama & Scale 177–83

wildflowers 24, 71–7

Winged everlasting (*Ammobium alatum*)
13, 45, 51

Winter Solstice 209–15

Wood spurge (*Euphorbia amygdaloides*) *66*

Woodland germander (*Teucrium
scorodonia*) *75*

Wormwood 69

wreaths: *Verdant Wreath* 151–5

Y

Yarrow (*Achillea*) *27*, 69

year-round harvesting 25

Yellow dock (*Rumex crispus*) 76, 88

Yorkshire fog (*Holcus lanatus*) 89

Z

Zinnia elegans 57

Published in 2022 by Hardie Grant Books,
an imprint of Hardie Grant Publishing

Hardie Grant Books (London)
5th & 6th Floors
52–54 Southwark Street
London SE1 1UN

Hardie Grant Books (Melbourne)
Building 1, 658 Church Street
Richmond, Victoria 3121

hardiegrantbooks.com

All rights reserved. No part of this publication may be reproduced,
stored in a retrieval system or transmitted in any form by any means,
electronic, mechanical, photocopying, recording or otherwise, without
the prior written permission of the publishers and copyright holders.

The moral rights of the author have been asserted.

Copyright text © Bex Partridge
Copyright photography © Laura Edwards
Self-Modern Regular and Italic © Lucas Le Bihan

British Library Cataloguing-in-Publication Data. A catalogue record
for this book is available from the British Library.

Flowers Forever
ISBN: 9781784884345

10 9 8 7 6 5 4 3 2 1

Publisher and Commissioner: Kajal Mistry
Editor: Kate Burkett
Design and Art Direction: Clare Newsam
Font: Dia (Schick Toikka) & Self Modern (Bretagne)
Photographer: Laura Edwards
Photographer assistant: Matthew Hague
Copy-editor: Emma Bastow
Proofreader: Caroline West
Indexer: Cathy Heath
Production Controller: Katie Jarvis

Colour reproduction by p2d
Printed and bound in China by Leo Paper Products Ltd